Instructional Analysis and Materials Development

Carl R. Bartel

Professor, Industrial Technical Education
Division of Technology
Arizona State University

 AMERICAN TECHNICAL SOCIETY CHICAGO, ILL. 60637

PREFACE

Effective instruction in any setting is dependent on many factors, one of which is the preparation of appropriate and relevant instructional materials. The instructional materials, which are developed for educational institutions and training agencies, are usually in the form of a comprehensive course of study or training plan.

The course of study or training plan should be based upon a carefully planned, organized, and conducted analysis procedure. This analysis procedure may be used for the identification and selection of learning tasks in any subject matter area and for any level of instruction.

To be more assured that the analysis is carried out efficiently, and that an appropriate course of study or training plan will result, a systematic approach is used. The systematic approach, including feedback provisions and a set of sequential components, will result in a usable set of instructional material when completed. A functional course of study or training plan will be obtained when following a systematic approach.

This book is divided into the three parts: Preparation and Description, Identification and Selection, and Development and Application. The three parts are presented in such a way that the student can move from a position of having very little knowledge about analysis and instructional material development to the completion of a comprehensive course of study or training plan designed for a specific instructional setting.

The approach followed in this book and the content and illustrations presented are based on many years of planning, developing, and offering courses for the preparation of industrial and technical instructors and trainers in education, industry, business, and governmental agencies.

Carl R. Bartel

TABLE OF CONTENTS

iv

035251

PART III   DEVELOPMENT AND APPLICATION

Part I
Preparation
And Description

chapter 1

A Systematic Plan

Appropriate planning and organization are essential in the development of instructional materials so that the most effective learning will occur. This planning and organization should take the form of a "systems approach," which includes the conduct of an instructional analysis through to the completion of a course of study or training plan.

Various systematic approaches have been used for many years to accomplish such things as identifying and sequencing specific steps in performing a job, essential topics to be covered in an after dinner speech, the sequential steps in assembling a kit, and procedures to follow in solving a laboratory problem. By adapting the systems approach, it can be effectively used to provide guidelines and check points in the development of instructional materials for educational and training purposes.

A systems approach includes an instructional analysis as one of its major segments which provides an inventory of tasks that form the basis for up-to-date outlines, guides, courses of study, and training plans. Developing and following a systematic plan causes one to be aware of the considerations that must be taken into account when preparing new courses and training programs. The use of the systems approach, including the instructional analysis, provides a more scientifically oriented procedure to be followed in the development of relevant materials.

A systematic plan for instructional materials and program development is presented in this chapter. The plan will apply and can be adapted to any content area, at any instructional level, and for any course regardless of its major function or purpose. The systematic plan as presented in this chapter contains a number of components and sub-components. By following the system as presented, more relevant materials will be developed and greater effectiveness of instruction should result. The three topics presented in this chapter are: (1) Systems Approach, (2) System Components, and (3) Systems and Materials Development.

CHAPTER OBJECTIVES

Through the study of this chapter and the completion of the suggested questions and activities, you will have accomplished the following objectives. You will be able to:

1. Explain the meaning of "systems approach" as it applies to analysis and instructional material development.
2. Sketch a systematic plan, identifying the specific components and showing their relationship, for the development of instructional materials for a specific instructional area.
3. List and describe the essential sub-components included in each component, explain how each might be developed, and describe their interrelationship.

SYSTEMS APPROACH

A "system" might be thought of as a number of interacting components that have a relationship to each other in such a way that a change in one component changes the others. A functioning system requires that each of its components must contribute its share; that is, each component has a role to play and if it is not carried out as planned, the total program will reflect the error. Therefore, each component of a system, when properly executed, will form a finished product acceptable to the user and the recipient, the instructor and the learner.

The systems approach for conducting an instructional analysis and the designing of a course of study or training plan provides an orderly process of gathering, analyzing, and selecting required tasks and support materials necessary for the preparation of a relevant course of study or training plan, as well as its conduct and its evaluation for effectiveness. The systems approach is based upon the assumption that the required behavior changes resulting from the completion of learning tasks can be identified, analyzed, and evaluated. The systems approach in instructional materials development also requires that appropriate performance objectives are written, instructional materials selected and/or developed, the proper instructional strategies followed, and the product evaluated by criterion testing.

The application of a systems approach helps to ensure that the interrelated components, or factors, are considered in the instructional materials development, and that the individuals completing the course or training program have developed skills to the level of proficiency stated in the performance objectives.

Sometimes a system is referred to as a "model" which is designed to explain, predict, or show relationships. Some may even prefer to use the term *strategy* or *stages* to represent an organized approach to instructional planning, instead of *system* or *model.* For sake of simplicity and clarity, the phrase "systems approach" will be used where interacting and interrelated components parts are placed together to attain a predetermined purpose.

The systems approach as dealt with in this book is a deliberately designed flow of activities called components which are interrelated and interacting for the purpose of attaining stated purposes as related to the overall goal of instructional materials development.

A very abbreviated form of a systems approach in the area of instructional materials development is illustrated in Figure 1-1.

The INPUT component is concerned with all those aspects dealing with identifying individuals who become involved in the system. It also includes the content selection and the environment required.

PROCESS includes the manner in which the content is presented, the resources, and the various approaches, strategies, methods, and techniques.

ABBREVIATED SYSTEMS APPROACH

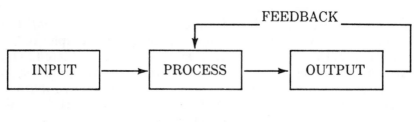

FIGURE 1-1

The third component, OUTPUT, deals with the product (learner) of the input and process. Evaluation of some sort is a very important part of this component. A feedback route is provided for those output learners who did not meet the minimum requirements, whatever these requirements may be.

Another abbreviated systems approach to analysis and instructional materials development, Figure 1-2, is composed of three major stages. These stages are: (1) Preparation and Description, (2) Identification and Selection, and (3) Development and Application.

The three stage system shown in Figure 1-2 is used as a basis for the systems approach presented and followed in this book. Each of the stages involve a number of specific components that need to be performed to effect appropriate selection and development of content.

THREE STAGE SYSTEMS APPROACH

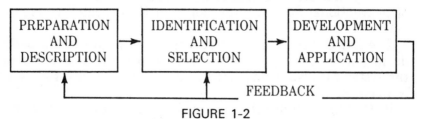

FIGURE 1-2

The first stage, *Preparation and Description,* is concerned with the approach to be followed in developing a course of study or training program. It deals with background information necessary before beginning the actual instructional material development. This stage includes those considerations such as philosophy of education and training, instructional areas that might be involved as well as the components of an instructional program. This stage places emphasis on establishing a justification for and general procedure to use in developing a selected course of study or training program.

Identification and Selection, the second stage, includes all of those activities dealing with the identification, selection and sequencing of content to be used in specific educational or training offerings. An inventory of tasks is developed during this stage using research techniques. Following the selection of specific tasks, each is sequenced, detailed and performance standards established for future use in presentation. Also, this stage involves the writing of performance requirements for the tasks selected.

Development and Application is the third and culminating stage of the three stage system. Here the content selected is organized in instructional order to fit particular student and instructor needs. Instructional schedules, lesson and session plans, written instruction sheets, and evaluation procedures are identified, selected, and/or developed. This stage also includes the selection of teaching aids and strategies and their application based on accepted practices and theories of learning.

Although this systems approach is applied to course of study and training plan development in this book, it must be emphasized that it also applies equally well, with possibly some adaptation, to curriculum development at any level and for any field of study. The principles of instructional materials development apply essentially to any length of session, course, training period, or curriculum.

Each of the components is briefly described in the next major section of this chapter and their relationships explained regarding the function to the total system. The chapters in this book are sequenced and treat most of the components as presented in the system.

SYSTEM COMPONENTS

The three stage system approach as presented in Figure 1-2 is comprised of ten specific components as shown in Figure 1-3. Following the ten component sequence will aid the developer in preparing a more relevant course of study or training program. Each of the components contains a number of subcomponents which, when completed, will cause the total system to function properly.

Each of the ten components that form the system are briefly described in the following pages. The descriptions are intended to show relationships between components, the need for the completion of one component before beginning the next, and the activities involved in each of the components. Eight of the ten components presented in Figure 1-3 are discussed in detail in the following chapters of this book.

Determine Scope and Limitations (1)

This component deals with the necessary considerations that need to be reviewed and evaluated before the course or training program developer begins the actual physical preparation of a course of study or training plan. First, it is important to be aware of already existing and available training and educational offerings similar to the ones being proposed so that excessive duplication can be avoided. It is also essential to determine if there is really a need for the proposed offering as evidenced by the consumers who will employ and use the products (students) who will be completing the particular course or training program.

Education and training philosophy must be considered before development of instructional materials begins. This includes the philosophy under which the institution or agency operates, as well as the philosophy of the course or training program developer and the instructor. Not only must the philosophy be considered, but also the overall goals which are within the framework of the philosophy so that a sense of direction is identified.

Each course that is developed represents a segment of one of the instructional areas found in education. The developer

A SYSTEMS APPROACH TO INSTRUCTIONAL
MATERIALS DEVELOPMENT

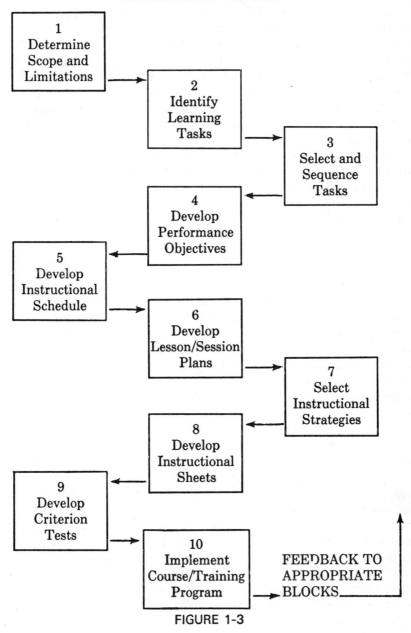

FIGURE 1-3

must have a clear understanding of the various instructional areas, especially the one in which the course becomes a part. This includes the principles, purposes, and overall goals of the instructional area and the relationships that exist.

Instructional materials such as courses of study and training plans consist of a number of components, each of which is related and yet unique by itself. It is essential that the importance, use, and purpose of each of the components be known so that effective programs of study, curriculums, courses of study or training plans, course outlines, and course guides can be developed.

Chapter 2 of this book treats this component of the system in the necessary detail so that more effective instructional materials will result.

Identify Learning Tasks (2)

System component 2, Identify Learning Tasks, deals with the identification of possible content to be considered for inclusion in the proposed course or training program. Before the actual identification takes place, however, certain analysis terms and procedures must be completely understood to avoid confusion.

Instructional developers employed by public or private educational agencies, or by business or industry training departments, must understand the definitions and usage of such terms and phrases as instructional analysis, inventory of tasks, duties or divisions, tasks, task steps, jobs, and positions. The terminology presented in Chapter 3 is that which is currently used by private and public institutions and agencies where instructional materials are being developed. The terminology is also acceptable by those representing the various instructional areas.

The actual identification of course or training program content (learning tasks) is probably the most important component in the system. Tentative usable learning tasks are identified, following a very structured sequence, to help assure that relevant and up-to-date content will be included in specific courses of study or training plans. The inventory of tasks, which have been tentatively identified through the use of a questionnaire or interview form, must go through a verifying procedure so that students will be learning content of most value to them and their employer or future employers.

An accepted procedure for selecting content (learning tasks) in the various instructional areas includes the following twelve steps: (1) identify scope and limitations, (2) review resource materials, (3) develop preliminary duty/division and task list, (4) conduct observations, (5) review by experts, (6) revise inventory, (7) pilot run, (8) finalize revision of inventory, (9) select sample of respondents, (10) administer inventory, (11) record and tabulate data, and (12) organize and interpret data.

The twelve steps listed above, and the various formats and procedures used to carry out each step, are presented and detailed in Chapter 4.

Select and Sequence Tasks (3)

Specific tasks are selected and sequenced following the development of the inventory of tasks and the task verification conducted through the use of the questionnaire or interview format. The responses to the inventory of tasks received by selected individuals need to be accurately tabulated and interpreted so that pertinent tasks may be selected for specific courses or training programs.

When the inventory of tasks has been verified, based upon responses to the questionnaires and/or interviews, criteria are established to be used for selecting those learning tasks most appropriate for the course or training program under development. The criteria may include such items as frequency of use, importance, complexity, time available, basic requirements and immediacy. Various formats and procedures are used to expedite the selection of appropriate learning tasks. These include analysis charts and outline formats.

After the instructor has selected those tasks thought essential for a particular offering, the sequencing procedure of the tasks begins. Many factors must be considered in the process of the sequencing of learning tasks. A knowledge of learning theory, as well as a knowledge of the practices followed by practitioners, will be of crucial importance for the instructor in sequencing the learning tasks. Various procedures are followed in the sequencing of tasks which include the use of assorted cards, analysis charts and outlines. The sequence of tasks comes only after the appropriate ones have been identified for a specific offering and for designated students.

Quite frequently the tasks are detailed soon after they have been identified and sequenced. This is done to provide additional data for the writing of performance objectives, writing of lesson or session plans, and the development of written instructional sheets.

Chapter 5 presents in detail the approaches, formats, and procedures, in tabulating data, selecting and sequencing tasks, and the detailing of each of the tasks.

Develop Performance Objectives (4)

Accountability is a part of any systems approach and should especially be a part of a system designed for the development of instructional materials. The writing of appropriate performance objectives for selected content provides the student and the instructor with a more organized presentation approach and evaluation procedure.

The accurate selection and sequencing of learning tasks are critical to course and training program development. However, unless a standard of achievement is also developed and applied, the outcomes will always be questionable. As soon as the learning tasks have been selected and sequenced, pertinent performance objectives are written.

Performance objectives are developed and written in student terms so that they know what is expected and what learning should take place. Performance objectives differ from goals in that they are specific and relate to selected task(s) within particular courses or training programs. Goals deal with broad concepts and relate to total divisions, units, and courses or training programs.

Every performance objective consists of a number of component parts which aid in making it more understandable and usable for evaluation purposes. The components include the identification of the students involved, the behavior to be exhibited by the student, the conditions under which the behavior takes place, and the standard which the performance must meet. Each course or training program should have sets of performance objectives written for the various divisions or units, and in turn for each of the sessions that are to be held.

Content dealing with the need for, use of, and development of performance objectives is presented in Chapter 6.

Develop Instructional Schedule (5)

Organization of the selected tasks is essential so that instruction and learning can progress in an orderly manner both for the student and the instructor. The development of an instructional schedule, which is a format for organizing the selected tasks, provides a means or vehicle which when used will assist the instructor in being more adequately prepared for the teaching responsibility.

The instructional schedule includes a sequential listing of all the content for any one selected course or training program. It provides a format for including the identification of all aids, devices, methods, etc., which will be used during the course or training program. It is possible for the instructional schedule to serve as a very abbreviated form of course or training program. However, its major purpose is to show relationships between all activities, aids, devices, and learning tasks included in a course.

Each instructional schedule format should contain a number of component parts which will cause it to be more usable. These include the course or program title, division or duty identification, selected tasks, time element, methods to be used, supporting aids, student activities, instruction sheet listing, text and references for study, and a listing of evaluation devices.

Chapter 7 describes the instructional schedule in detail and provides a number of examples that might be used.

Develop Lesson and Session Plans (6)

Following the identification and sequencing of the learning tasks, the writing of performance objectives, and the completion of all entries in the instructional schedule, the lesson or session planning begins. The lesson or session plan actually helps to bring all the previous planning into focus so that the identified tasks can be learned.

There are a great number of reasons why lesson or session

plans should be prepared. Some of these are that they provide a logical presentation sequence and some standardization, a record of accomplishment and basis for revision, and provide continuity for the total course or training program.

Lesson and session plans are developed for specific courses or training programs and include a limited number of learning tasks. They must be designed to meet the needs of the students based on the content under consideration. The plan has as its basis the detailed learning tasks. Lesson and session plans should be developed to cover a logical segment (tasks) rather than be based solely on the time factor such as specific number of minutes, hours, or sessions.

The most effective lesson and session plans make use of a five step approach which includes the following: (1) introduction, (2) presentation, (3) application, (4) summary, and (5) evaluation. The other components of a lesson or session plan include course identification, lesson title, lesson objectives, supporting aids and devices, and assignments.

A structured procedure should be followed when writing lesson and session plans to be sure that a comprehensive and workable plan results. Chapter 8 presents the importance, use, components, and writing procedure for developing the lesson or session plan.

Select Instructional Strategies (7)

This component includes the selection of appropriate methods and techniques used by the instructor to present the content, the learning tasks that were identified earlier for the specific course or training program. It also includes the selection and/or development of the audio and visual aids used to support the instructor's presentations.

Although the course content may be accurately identified, sequenced, and organized, it will not be effective unless the instructor provides the right environment and opportunities for the students to learn the content. Different content from the various instructional areas require different presentation methods and techniques, as well as various types of audio and visual aids. The level of the content and the background abilities of the students also require differing methods, techniques, and relevant aids.

One of the major concerns is that regardless of the method, technique or aid selected, it must be presented or used so that maximum student involvement results. This requires that active approaches such as case studies, role playing, demonstrations and questioning techniques should be planned for and used.

Instructional strategies, the selection and development of teaching methods, techniques, and audio/visual aids, are not treated in this book. These professional teacher education areas include a broad list of competencies which are very adequately covered in other texts and are offered as separate courses in most colleges and universities.

Develop Instructional Sheets (8)

The eighth component of the instructional materials system, Develop Instruction Sheets, is one designed to provide supporting materials containing content which is not readily available through texts, references and other commercially prepared materials. A major characteristic of the written instruction sheet is that it is instructor prepared and instructor used, and is designed for particular course and training programs. Instruction sheets are prepared only when other existing appropriate materials are not available.

Instructor prepared written instruction sheets are essential to help clarify concepts, present new ideas and skills, and to reinforce what has already been presented. Instruction sheets do not take the place of the instructor. Rather, instruction sheets provide for individualization and assist in presentations when working with large classes. They also place the responsibility on the students for learning and provide a student with the opportunity to develop self reliance as a result of their use. Instruction sheets are difficult to write. Unfortunately, many instructors do not have the time or ability to write effective ones. The effective use of instruction sheets is dependent upon the instructor's ability as well as the student's ability to read.

All instructor prepared instruction sheets can be grouped into the three classifications of: (1) assignment sheets, (2) procedure sheets, and (3) information sheets. The assignment sheet can be either manipulative or informational and is one designed to assist students in completing a particular assignment which emphasizes a great amount of student involvement. Procedure sheets are developed and used when a specific and structured procedure is to be followed. It, too, can be either manipulative or information oriented. The information sheets are designed to present information and facts that help explain the why, when, and where about the content under consideration.

Written instruction sheets should be designed to be as self-instructional as possible. This requires that the sheet must include all relevant data and information so that students can use them with very little assistance from the instructor. Chapter 9 presents the importance, uses, kinds, criteria, and writing suggestions for the development of instruction sheets.

Develop Criterion Tests (9)

This particular component could be completed earlier in the system, following the component on developing performance objectives. However, by placing it as the ninth component, an advantage is gained in that the various activities, problems, techniques, and procedures have been identified and are ones that will provide additional input for the development of criterion tests.

Criterion evaluation is where the progress of a student is compared with some predetermined objective standard. This is in contrast to norm evaluation where evaluation of progress is made on the basis of comparing a student's achievement with other students' achievement in the same or like course or training program. Criterion evaluation or testing requires that the appropriate performance objectives have been written. The performance objectives are the basis for all testing and evaluation in a criterion evaluation system.

Testing and evaluating procedures are used not only to assign grades but also to evaluate instructor performance, identify learning problems, and provide a means where students have knowledge of progress regarding their competency. An appropriate evaluation procedure plays a major role in providing feedback to the instructor regarding the relevancy of the course or training program. It serves as one of the considerations for use in revising the course or training program content.

All types of content must be evaluated, including content that is manipulative, informational, and attitudinal. Various formats, procedures, and devices are used for this type of evaluation, including objective tests, subjective tests, performance tests and rating scales. If the performance objectives have been correctly written, the form, procedure, and devices used for evaluation will automatically be determined.

This component is not presented in this book since very adequate professional teacher education books and materials on this subject are readily available. Also, testing and evaluation is generally treated as a separate course in most colleges and universities.

Implement Course/Training Program (10)

The instructor must be careful that in the process of completing the various components, that each component does not become a separate and unrelated entity when compared with the other components. Physically, the course of study or training plan should be assembled so that it can be easily used, which means that the individual components and sections form a unified program.

Learning theory and teaching techniques must be considered so that the content included in the course of study or training plan can be presented in a most effective manner. The instructor must always keep in mind that each group of students is different from the last group, regarding their abilities, interests and goals. This requires that varying approaches will need to be used over the years even though the content may stay relatively the same.

The instructor should make every effort to individualize the instruction regardless of the level, abilities, or number of students involved in the content. Individualization actually requires more time, effort, and organization on the instructor's part than the more traditional approaches. However, evidence indicates that for many students an individual approach is more efficient as well as more effective.

Each course and training program must be evaluated during and after it is initiated. The form of evaluation varies with the kind of students, level, and content, as well as the policy of the institution or agency providing the offering. Feedback of various forms is essential and should be used for continual revision of the developed instructional materials.

Application procedures and instructional proactives are presented and described in Chapter 10 of this book. This is the last component of the system and if carried out will help the instructor to maintain an up-to-date and relevant course or training program.

SYSTEMS AND MATERIALS DEVELOPMENT

The course or training program analyzer and developer needs to be aware of, knowledgeable about, and able to apply the systematic approach to instructional materials development. Some justifiable reasons for following a systematic plan in the development of instructional materials (courses of study and training plans) include the following:

1. Effective instruction and lasting retention don't just happen; they result from having materials organized in a logical and psychological sequence.
2. Well prepared and sequenced instructional materials provide a basis for critical review and evaluation by the instructor, learners, and supervisors.
3. Systematically developed instructional materials better serve as a ledger to which additions and deletions can and should be made—a technical update.
4. They provide greater assurance to those concerned that relevant content is being considered and taught in an organized manner.
5. A systematic plan helps to provide a guide for assisting the instructor in planning and conducting each specific session.
6. It helps to provide a ready reference regarding the total scope and content of the course or training plan being presented.

7. The plan allows for arranging content material so learning progresses rapidly and effectively.
8. It causes the instructor to think through the content, how it was developed, and the direction in which the course should go.
9. It assists in keeping the goals and objectives to be attained clearly in the forefront along with the activities proposed to accomplish them.
10. A systematic approach definitely aids when an attempt is made to correlate content with other subject areas.

A critical issue that must be considered during the early stages of instructional materials development is that of who has the responsibility for developing materials to be used by instructors. This is especially true when considering beginning instructors. In some cases, in the past, the practice was for the supervisor to provide some form of course of study or training session format which had been detailed to some extent. On the surface, this appeared to be an appropriate and acceptable practice. However, in most cases instructors not only resent being told exactly what and how to teach, but in many cases have a difficult time interpreting the materials given them that have been developed by someone else. To force an instructor to follow a prescribed, highly detailed course of study or training plan is not practical or effective.

An effective, detailed course of study or training plan cannot be prepared by a committee or group of subject experts. They can develop some guidelines and, in some instances, outlines, but not all the detailed materials to be used for a particular course with specific groups of individuals.

An effective course of study or training plan is tailor-made for specific groups to be served. With this in mind, then, it must be the individual instructor's responsibility for the preparation of the detailed and comprehensive course of study or training plan. The instructor has the responsibility to obtain the input from others, i.e., supervisors, fellow instructors and learners, but it remains the instructor's responsibility to put the package together. A single instructor has the responsibility for a specific course which is developed for a local situation to meet specific learner needs.

The course of study or training plan, it must be remembered, is not a rigid document, rather it must remain flexible. This means that it must be ever changing, reflecting the changes in the technology, the learner needs, and incorporating the up-to-date theories and practices of learning and teaching.

SUMMARY

The use of a systematic approach in the development of instructional materials helps to assure a more up-to-date and relevant course of study or training plan. A system consists of a number of interacting components that have a relationship to each other in such a way that a change in one component causes changes in the others. The use of a systems approach provides for the orderly process of gathering, analyzing, selecting, and sequencing required tasks and support materials necessary for the preparation of a relevant course of study or training plan.

A three stage system approach meets the requirements for developing instructional materials. The stages are: (1) Preparation and Description, (2) Identification and Selection, and (3) Development and Application. Ten major components are included in the three stages.

Stage 1, *Preparation and Description,* includes the component of Determine Scope and Limitations. It is concerned with the background information necessary for initiating the course of study or training plan development.

Identification and Selection, the second stage, is concerned with the identification, selection, sequencing, and performance requirements of the content. This stage includes the components of Identify Learning Tasks, Select and Sequence Tasks, and Develop Performance Objectives.

The third stage of the systems approach, *Development and Application,* includes the components of Develop Instructional Schedules, Develop Lesson and Session Plans, Select Instructional Strategies, Develop Instruction Sheets, Develop Criterion Tests, and Implement Course/Training Program. This stage is a culminating stage and is concerned with organizing and further development of the selected content. It includes the strategies for more effective teaching and learning.

A course or training program developed following a systematic approach provides such advantages as more effective learning and teaching, a ledger of presentations and accomplishments, greater relevancy and increased effectiveness in organizing. The development of a comprehensive detailed course of study is the responsibility of the individual instructor. The course of study and training plan must be developed as a flexible document, one which needs to be continually revised for it to be effective.

SUGGESTED QUESTIONS AND ACTIVITIES

1. Explain what is meant by a systems approach as applied to instructional materials development.

2. What relationship does evaluation and criterion testing have to the total systems approach?

3. A three stage systems approach was presented. Briefly explain the make-up of each stage and the major functions included.

4. The first component of the system presented is *Determine Scope and Limitations.* Make a list of individuals, groups, associations, and agencies that you will contact to obtain information to complete this component.

5. *Develop Performance Objectives* is the fourth component of the system. Discuss reasons why this component should not appear as a later component. Would it be better if it was the second component? Explain.

6. Present a number of reasons why the development of written instruction sheets occurs after the development of instructional schedules.

7. *Select Instructional Strategies* is the seventh component. Could this component be accomplished earlier in the system? Explain.

8. List a number of ways or procedures that might be used in evaluating the effectiveness of courses of study and training plans.

9. Develop a list of reasons why the systems approach for course of study and training plan development should be used.

10. Based upon the study of this chapter and other related references, develop a tentative system which you plan to follow in developing your course of study or training plan.

chapter 2

Education and Training

The use of a systematic approach to instructional materials development will more nearly provide current and relevant courses of study and training plans. However, before the development of instructional materials takes place, the analyzer and course developer must obtain an adequate understanding of education and training philosophy as it relates to the instructional area under consideration, as well as the components of instructional materials which will form the eventual course of study or training plan.

An instructional offering is very seldom developed and presented in isolation. The developer must be aware of the relationship that exists between philosophy held and instructional areas included in the fields of education and training. This knowledge will assist in identifying, selecting, and sequencing content for more effective learning.

This chapter, which is part of the first stage in the systems approach to instructional materials development, provides a base from which the developer of materials can begin to identify, select, sequence learning tasks, and develop courses of study or training plans. The following topics are included: (1) Education and Training Philosophy, (2) Instructional Areas, and (3) Instructional Materials Components.

CHAPTER OBJECTIVES

Through the study of this chapter and the completion of suggested questions and activities, you will have accomplished the following objectives. You will be able to:

1. Define philosophy and explain its importance and use when developing instructional materials.
2. Describe the relationship between the instructor's philosophy and the observable performance, and list some typical concepts that industrial education and training instructors hold.
3. Define and explain terms used to designate selected instructional areas, list the purposes of each, and graphically show the relationship between these areas.
4. Define selected instructional material development components and graphically show the relationship between each of them.
5. Describe the importance and use of the course of study in the instructional program.

EDUCATION AND TRAINING PHILOSOPHY

For an effective analysis and course of study or training plan development, the instructor must have an understanding of philosophy as it relates to education and training and to the particular courses included.

Philosophy of a school or agency, as well as that of the instructor, can be seen in the way the offerings are conducted, people are treated, and courses or training programs are presented. The philosophy held by schools, agencies, and individuals may be thought of as fundamental beliefs, concepts, and attitudes regarding the activities and programs under consideration.

It is imperative that one has a philosophy about education and training before embarking on an analysis and a course of study or training plan development venture. It is most important that the instructional materials be developed within the overall framework of the respective agency's or school's philosophy. This means that developers of instructional materials must be cognizant of the prevailing philosophy and the relationship of this philosophy to that of the instructor's. In the final analysis, the philosophy of the institution or agency must be reviewed and studied before a course of study or training plan can be developed and effectively used.

The philosophy of a particular institution or agency provides the direction in which it wants its educational and training plans to move. A poorly defined philosophy will cause an inadequate educational and training offering. If the philosophy of the employing agency is to provide a general orientation to the learners, then the content and emphasis of the courses of study and training plans will or should reflect that approach. However, if the philosophy dictates skill training, then the emphasis must be oriented to specific job preparation, making the training plan content highly specific and closely related to the actual jobs for which the learners are preparing. In many cases the philosophy of an educational institution will be primarily that of the transmission of cultural heritage as well as the meeting of individual needs. Most institutions, as well as many training agencies, hold the philosophy that includes the meeting of individual and society needs involving general as well as the vocational aspects.

The institution or training agency does dictate, directly or indirectly, the direction in which a course or training plan is to move. This is determined by the individuals who are in the policy making position, and to some extent, by the persons who are developing the specific course of study and training plan. The instructor, therefore, must understand and realize in what kind of framework or philosophy in which the course or training program will be offered. Many situations are not ideal and, therefore, an instructor's philosophy about what education and training should be, does vary from that of his/ her employer. Of major concern, however, is that the instructor and the employing agency must have an interest in and make a concerted effort to meet the needs of the individuals involved, and the community and the society in general.

Philosphy And The Instructor

The direction which a certain course of study or training plan takes is expressed by the stated purposes which, in a sense, are an expression of the philosophy in terms understandable to the general public. The purpose of any course of study or training plan reflects the philosophy about education and training the institution, agency, or individual holds, whether expressed as a philosophy or not.

An instructor must be aware that a philosophy deals with

laws, principles, beliefs, concepts, and attitudes, which will govern the lives and acts in a particular environment. The instructor's as well as the institution's or agency's philosophy does, therefore, make a great difference as to the kinds, amount, and relevancy of learning that takes place.

An instructor's philosophy represents the beliefs, it governs the approach to the course and training plan development. It actually governs the approach to teaching. The way the course is met, instructed, critiqued, and conducted reflects the instructor's philosophy. One can readily identify an instructor who is student oriented or subject matter oriented by the way the class moves along. Although a person's philosophy and beliefs tend to remain somewhat the same over the years, they are not static. Not only does an institution and agency's philosophy regarding educational training change but also a particular instructor's philosophy changes. However, this tends to occur rather slowly. Even though an instructor's basic beliefs and attitudes change slowly, they do change, reflecting experiences and the environment in which the instructor is working and living.

Some Typical Concepts Held

Instructors who are people oriented and emphasize the providing of learning opportunities to their students tend to hold some typical concepts. These, in the main, reflect their philosophy. These concepts are as follows:

1. Education and various forms of training must be continuous, from birth on.
2. A person must have an opportunity to receive appropriate and balanced education and training, which include a broad general orientation adequate exploration, and specific job preparation. The level at which these are offered change with the individual as well as the nature of the content.
3. All seekers should have an equal opportunity for education and training. The abilities of learners should be assessed and programs developed to meet their specific needs.
4. Courses and training sessions, in the majority of

cases, should be so structured as to not only permit but encourage experimentation and provide for the element of creativity.
5. Adaptability should be built into each offering which encourages a broad scope approach and aids in social as well as economic mobility.
6. Content for course of study and training plan development should be selected so as to provide that educational and training content which is not readily available to the learner or trainee in the real world of work.

A philosophy, whether listed by an institution, agency, or individual, is developed and stated for a number of very good reasons, which include:

1. It gives needed direction for the instructional offering.
2. It provides necessary and needed guidelines for the instructor as well as the employer.
3. It provides a framework within which the purposes, goals, and objectives can be developed.

A relationship does exist between philosophy, goals, and objectives. In fact, they interact and are dependent upon each other. This relationship, between philosophy, goals and objectives, is illustrated in Figure 2-1.

A RELATIONSHIP

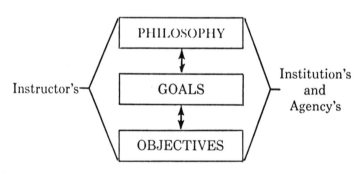

FIGURE 2-1

Goal statements are broad and are often found listed for programs, curriculums and subject areas, whereas objectives are more specific and are used to indicate what will be accomplished through courses and their units and divisions, or through training plans and their individual training sessions.

A more detailed discussion of goals and objectives, as these relate to analysis, course of study or training plan development is presented in Chapter 6.

INSTRUCTIONAL AREAS

To help provide a base so that an appropriate analysis and course of study or training plan can be developed, a selected number of terms representing instructional areas are described, including the principles and purposes of each. It is important for the analyzer and course of study or training plan developer to know the relationships among and between these instructional areas to help clarify the place of the instructional area and course in the educational continuum. A more comprehensive treatment of these instructional areas and others that are closely related may be found in reference material specifically devoted to their interpretation.

The following instructional areas will be considered:

1. Career Education
2. Practical Arts Education
3. Vocational (Occupational) Education
4. Industrial Education
5. Industrial Arts Education
6. Vocational Industrial Education
7. Industrial Technical Education

Career Education

Career education as practiced today is a concept rather than an instructional area or a course or program offering. However, it is treated here because of its relationship to the other instructional areas. The effects of career education should be felt at all levels of education, from early childhood through adult life. It provides an opportunity for individuals to learn to live more effectively in their chosen environment, it provides them an opportunity to explore possible vocations and professions, and finally, it presents individuals with the opportunity to participate in up-to-date courses and training sessions designed to prepare them for chosen jobs and occupations.

Career education includes an orientation to the world of work as it is today and as it is projected for the future. It provides for broad exploration of the current occupational clusters as well as some in-depth exploration in selected clusters, based on selections made by the individuals themselves. It also provides for eventual preparation in more specific clusters and occupations. The levels at which each of these occur depend somewhat on the individuals, their backgrounds and needs, as well as the available offerings and facilities.

Career education is not a separate type of educational program but rather a concept that prevails in all education. It might be thought of as a revitalization of the General Education as found in many of our public schools today. Figure 2-2 illustrates the concept of career education and its components of orientation, exploration and preparation.

CAREER EDUCATION CONCEPT

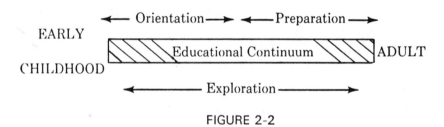

FIGURE 2-2

Orientation, exploration, and preparation, as shown, overlap. The extent depends upon the needs of the individual. Usually, however, the orientation takes place during the elementary school years. The exploration phase most often takes place during middle and secondary school years, and the preparation stage occurs at the upper secondary and post secondary level. It must be remembered, however, that the orientation and exploration phase of career education may occur at all levels.

Actually, career education is an all encompassing concept in which many programs, including those that are more related to the industrial sector of our world of work, are involved. Figure 2-3 shows the relationship of the instructional areas of practical arts, vocational (occupational) education, industrial arts, industrial technical education, vocational industrial

INSTRUCTIONAL AREAS

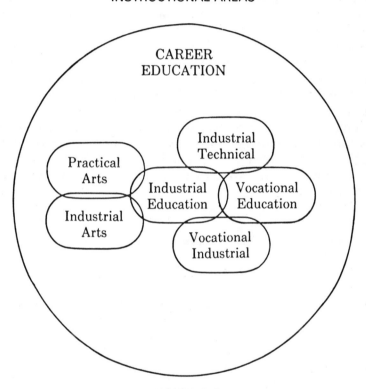

FIGURE 2-3

education, and industrial education as part of the total career education concept. It will be noted that industrial education actually includes the three instructional areas of industrial arts (general orientation), industrial technical education (vocational orientation), and vocational industrial education (vocational orientation). It can be seen from this why a considerable amount of confusion exists when the term of industrial education is used to describe an instructional area.

Practical Arts Education

Practical arts education is an umbrella term which includes a number of instructional areas which are activity oriented and have a general education emphasis, providing learning that is necessary and applicable to all regardless of an individual's ultimate goal. Often the instructional areas included in practical arts have a heavy emphasis on manipulative activity, however, not with the sole emphasis on occupational preparation.

Some of the typical instructional areas included in the practical arts category are industrial arts, home economics, general business, fine arts, and physical education. Experiences are provided that emphasize leisure time activities, consumer knowledge, development of useful manipulative skills, and an orientation to the world of work and world of living. Content classified as practical arts tends to more nearly meet the needs of learners than that which we have classified as general education, and is more relevant to current technology and practices.

Vocational (Occupational) Education

Vocational and occupational education offerings are specifically planned and designed to prepare individuals to enter into selected jobs, positions and occupations; as well as to provide upgrading skills for those who are already employed in the selected occupations. Vocational and occupational education is considered special interest education—planned and offered for those individuals who are interested in preparing or advancing themselves in selected jobs, in broad occupational areas, and in occupational clusters.

Vocational education is a part of the total educational, and particularly the career education, continuum. It includes offerings that are beyond the exploratory stage and are found usually at the senior and post high school level, and in industry, business, and military training programs.

Instructional areas classified within vocational or occupational education are not static programs. They are not static in nature and content. Rather, they do and should change as the technology itself changes and also as the individual's needs change. This creates a need for continual revision and updating of content which must be based on an appropriate analysis procedure.

Education classified as vocational or occupational education is perpetuated by the fact that people must be productive in some form and render useful services. Those who will not or cannot do this become a liability both to themselves and to society. Appropriately developed vocational and occupational offerings economize and conserve both human and natural resources.

Contrary to popular belief, vocational or occupational education is vitally concerned with the whole individual and the contribution to society. Vocational and occupational education provide individuals the opportunities to develop psychomotor, cognitive and affective skills so they can take their rightful place in society and assume responsibility beyond those only related to their selected occupation.

All individuals should have the opportunity to select the type, level, and depth of program most suitable to their needs and abilities and society's demands. However, those attending vocational and occupational offerings should have a required background so that they can benefit from the content presented. They should also have made a commitment to themselves and society as to their interest in following through the program to actual work in the area at a later date. In turn, individuals who have not made commitments should not be permitted to enroll in specialized vocational and occupational classes, which are usually much more expensive than other types of offering, and, therefore, would be a waste of both human and material resources.

The terms vocational and occupational education mean basically the same. However, the term *vocational* is used most frequently for secondary level offerings while the term *occupational* is used primarily at the post secondary level. Both terms are used to refer to instructional area offerings that lead to goals which may require pre-collegiate or college level instruction but not designed to lead specially to a four year professional degree.

Industrial Education

In the broad sense, industrial education applies to all types of education relating to industry. However, as it is used in educational planning and program development, it includes the instructional areas of industrial arts, industrial technical education and vocational industrial education.

Many institutions and agencies list their courses as industrial education. This has caused some confusion since one is not sure whether the offerings are general or vocational, or whether a combination is being attempted. As most industrial instructors realize, a general and vocational emphasis is an impossible function for one particular course to serve. To make efficient and effective use of resources, both human and material, courses as well as training sessions are developed to serve selected groups. If the major function of an offering is an orientation to the world of work, it will not then serve adequately those who desire skills for occupational preparation. Granted the content will not hurt them—in fact it will be beneficial. However, if job preparation is the goal, the course

INDUSTRIAL EDUCATION

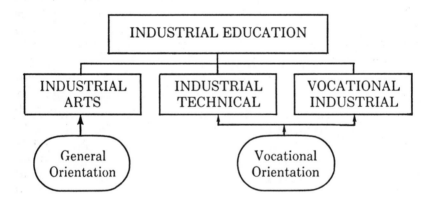

FIGURE 2-4

or training plan should be developed with that objective in mind.

Often the term industrial education is used by schools and universities as an umbrella term to indicate that two or three of the instructional areas (Industrial Arts, Vocational Industrial and Industrial Technical Education) are offered through a particular division or department. However, a specific course, especially if it is technical in content, should not be classified as industrial education. However, this is not necessarily true in the case of professional teacher education courses.

Non-professional teacher education offerings, courses and training sessions should not be classified as industrial education. They should be listed as either industrial arts, industrial technical, or vocational industrial. Figure 2-4 clearly shows the relationship and the orientation of each of the instructional areas included in the term industrial education.

Industrial Arts

Industrial arts is an instructional area which is non-vocational in purpose, but rather an area which provides a general education emphasis to experiences that are centered around our technological culture. Industrial arts is a part of the total educational program which provides individuals the opportunity to study about tools, materials, and processes relating to the industrial sector, as it functions today.

Industrial arts is the general education component of industrial education. It is offered and is found in the school system beginning at the Kindergarten level and extends through the University. At each of these levels it provides individuals with the opportunity to participate in a representative sampling of industrial skills and process. Industrial arts should be made available to all students regardless of their future chosen occupation. However, it has special significance to vocational industrial and industrial technical offerings as it may serve a prevocational purpose for these instructional areas.

Industrial arts is a vital segment of the career education concept. It has excellent guidance value in that it assists individuals to base their choices of future occupations on relevant experiences.

Some general assumptions made regarding the place and purpose of Industrial arts are:

1. Offerings should be open to all comers.
2. Offerings are non-vocational as a major purpose.
3. Offerings may serve prevocational and technical needs.
4. Content is based on current technology.
5. Student interests must be considered in content selection as well as content presentation.
6. Offerings should remain broad in nature, not highly specialized.

Vocational Industrial

Vocational industrial education (sometimes referred to as trade and industrial education), is a vocationally oriented instructional area offered at the secondary, post secondary and adult level in educational institutions and in industry and business. Vocational industrial courses are also offered by many private educational agencies.

Vocational industrial education offerings, in the main, emphasize the manipulative skill development, supported by relevant informational content. However, in some specific vocational industrial subject areas, the informational content occupies as much time and emphasis as does the manipulative content. Course offerings classified as vocational industrial provide students the opportunity to become highly proficient in the areas of fabrication, installation, production, and operation; using tools, equipment and materials.

Students served by vocational industrial programs and courses not only include full-time students at the secondary and post secondary level, but also apprentices, journeymen, industrial workers, service personnel and many more out-of-school youth and adults. Secondary vocational industrial offerings are usually designed to provide students with skills applicable to broad clusters of occupations. As one progresses to the post secondary and adult levels, the specificity of education and training in the vocational industrial education area increases. Individuals who complete vocational industrial courses at the secondary and post secondary level are considered to have attained sufficient skills to obtain jobs that are closely related to their instruction. However, they are not considered as finished or skilled journeymen or workers. Rather, they have gone through an appropriate learning stage and do have the skills necessary to obtain and hold a job; and with experience and further on-the-job training, will be considered as highly proficient workers in the field.

Some general assumptions made regarding the place and purpose of vocational industrial education are:

1. Course offerings are found in the upper grades of secondary schools, and at the post secondary and adult level.
2. Offerings are vocational in purpose.
3. Course content is selected from appropriate analysis made from jobs performed, positions held, and the changing technology itself.
4. Success in vocational industrial offerings usually requires above average manual dexterity and a high interest in application and fabrication.
5. Specificity of education and training increases as the level of the offerings increases.
6. Both the manipulative and informational content are emphasized based on the particular job or occupation for which the offering is designed.

Industrial Technical

Industrial technical education is a vocationally oriented instructional area offered primarily at the post secondary and adult level in educational institutions and in industry and business. Also, a great number of industrial technical courses and training sessions are found to be offered by private agencies.

Industrial technical education offerings are based on a sound background of science and mathematics with a heavy emphasis on the principles of the particular technology as applied to modern design, production, installation, and maintenance. Since industrial technical education, as an instructional area, is primarily post secondary, it depends upon other instructional areas to provide the basics or prerequisites needed by individuals who plan to enter the industrial technical courses and training programs.

Industrial technical programs and courses provide for broadly based competencies in the field of applied science providing the necessary skills for graduates who plan to obtain positions in one of the clusters of related work in the particular technical field. The industrial technical offerings are often quite formal and are of college level and intensity. Industrial technical offerings have a relationship to the counterpart professional offerings and the counterpart vocational industrial offerings. Probably in a majority of instances the industrial technical offerings tend to have a closer relationship to their counterpart professional programs (i.e., Electronic Technology-Electrical Engineering; Civil Technology-Civil Engineering). The graduate of an industrial technical program is considered as a liaison between the professional and the skilled worker.

Some general assumptions made regarding the place and purpose of industrial technical education are:

1. Course offerings are found at the post secondary level, of college level and intensity.
2. Offerings are vocational in purpose.
3. Content is selected from analysis of on-going technology.
4. All offerings are based on a sound background of mathematics and science.
5. Course content emphasizes application of scientific principles as they relate to the technology.
6. Students entering the program should be average or above in their scholastic work.
7. Offerings are designed to provide students with abilities in areas of research, design, development, testing, installation, and maintenance.

INSTRUCTIONAL MATERIALS COMPONENTS

A number of components must be considered and defined before conducting an analysis for purposes of instructional material development. Quite often these terms have been used interchangeably. However, each component is different but is interrelated and dependent on the others. Following are the components, their description, and the relationship that exists between them:

1. Program of Study
2. Curriculum
3. Course of Study (Training Plan)
4. Course Outline
5. Course Guide

Program of Study

A program of study is all encompassing and includes the total educational offerings of an institution or agency, as well as other activities, curricular and extra-curricular, which are supported by and under the supervision of the institution or agency. A program of study may be very broad or narrow, depending on a number of factors, some of which are the philosophy of the institution or agency, the facilities, and the competencies held by the personnel employed. Generally the secondary and post secondary educational institutions offer various programs of studies whch are designed to meet the needs of entering students regardless of their eventual goals.

Curriculum

A curriculum consists of an orderly arrangement or series of courses and supporting activities designed to help individuals reach a long range educational goal. A curriculum may be of any length. However, traditionally it is one to four years in length. Curriculums may be occupational, academic, general, or career oriented, depending upon the institution or agency offering it and the goal of the students enrolled in it. In the occupational fields, curriculums are designed to prepare individuals for job clusters as well as specific positions. Curriculums may be found to prepare individuals for positions in teaching, as electronic technicians, as firemen, as pilots, etc.

Course of Study/Training Plan

A course of study is a plan developed by the instructor which provides a total scope and sequence of content to be presented. The course of study may be very comprehensive which includes a listing of the specific content and *all* materials needed to teach and evaluate a course, or it may be very brief including only the content listing (tasks) and a general description of materials to be used. A comprehensive course of study is a complete blueprint of instruction for a particular segment of subject matter prepared by the instructor.

A comprehensive course of study or training plan usually contains the following components or sections:

1. General description
   a. Title
   b. Table of contents
   c. Introductory statement—including the nature and scope
   d. Grade level of instruction and length
   e. For whom intended
   f. Entrance requirements
   g. Methods, techniques, and procedures to be used
2. Organization and purpose
   a. Philosophy statement
   b. Goals and objectives
   c. Major duties or divisions
   d. Time limitations
3. Course content
   a. Sequential listing of learning tasks
   b. Instructional schedule, including the listing of tasks and all related support materials
   c. Performance objectives
   d. Lesson plans
4. Support materials
   a. Jobs, projects, activities, etc. (drawings, pictures, etc.)
   b. Resource materials: texts, references, etc.
   c. Audio-visual aids and charts
   d. Written instructional sheets
   e. Evaluation devices

The components of a comprehensive course of study or training plan in check sheet form, shown in Figure 2-5, may be used when developing a comprehensive course of study or training plan.

Figure 2-6 shows the relationship between the three component parts of an instructional program which have been

COURSE OF STUDY/TRAINING PLAN CHECK SHEET
Essential Components

The following are the major components to be included in a course of study/training plan.

_____ 1. Cover Page

_____ 2. Table of Contents

_____ 3. Introduction Section

      a. Course goals and purposes.

      b. Nature and scope of the course.

      c. Length of course and credit to be earned.

      d. Grade level and type of students served.

      e. Prerequisites and other entrance requirements.

_____ 4. Division Performance Objectives

_____ 5. Instructional Schedules to include:

      a. Sequential and classified listing of tasks (manipulative, informational, and attitudinal.)

      b. Sequential listing of projects, problems, experiments and/or activities.

      c. Sequential listing of supporting materials (texts and references, films, written instruction sheets, evaluation devices, charts, etc.)

_____ 6. Lesson Plans or Session Plans

_____ 7. Prepared Visual Aids

_____ 8. Written Instruction Sheets

_____ 9. Evaluative Devices

      a. Manipulative content—performance tests, rating scales, etc.

      b. Informational content—various types/kinds of test questions.

      c. Attitudinal content—rating and observational procedures.

_____10. List of texts and references, films, charts, booklets, etc., and their sources.

_____11. Progress records and/or charts.

_____12. Other support materials.

FIGURE 2-5

presented. As can be seen, the components are interrelated and will interact with each other in an on-going educational or training program.

INSTRUCTIONAL MATERIALS COMPONENTS

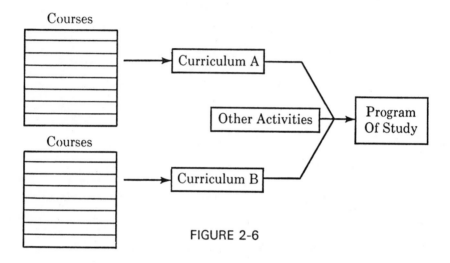

FIGURE 2-6

In the comprehensive form, a course of study or training plan shows the scope and sequence of content and activities for a particular subject or part of a subject. A comprehensively developed course of study or training plan enables the instructor to appraise the results more adequately, thus providing the opportunity to add to as well as reject materials. It serves as a ledger for recording changes, a chance to keep up-to-date, make notations, and adding and deleting. It provides the instructor the chance to avoid mistakes, to avoid undue overlap and costly omissions.

A well developed course of study or training plan provides assurances that something is actually being taught in some organized form. A course of study or training plan must be well planned and organized, but must remain flexible so that it will meet the changing needs of individuals and society.

Often the practice in the past was for the instructor to receive a course of study. Today, however, it is assumed that the responsibility for developing a course of study or training plan is that of the instructor. Often, however, the course of study or training plan is prepared from outlines or guides developed by other individuals and groups which have been given to the instructor by the supervisor, obtained from the district, or from some other sources.

Well developed courses of study or training plans serve the following purposes:

1. Assist in defining the scope and sequence of content to be covered.
2. Provide the instructor with a day-to-day guide for content presentation.
3. Provide opportunity for the arrangement of content into a logical as well as psychological plan for effective learning.
4. Provide a base from which an evaluation program and procedure can be established.
5. Provide a basis for the addition and deletion of content based on relevancy and need.
6. Aid in keeping course and training content in line with stated objectives.
7. Help in establishing a time frame and serve as a guide for possible changes.
8. Assist in the correlation of content with that of other subject and content areas.
9. Cause instructors to keep up-to-date and promote their professional development.

Course/Training Outline

The course outline is usually considered one of the first steps to be completed before a comprehensive course of study or training plan is developed. A course outline is actually a skeleton framework of a course of study or comprehensive training plan and is most often developed by the individual instructor for his use. However, a course or training plan developer may use someone else's outline as a base from which to develop his course of study or training plan. The course outline may or may not be based on an analysis. Usually it is developed from other materials already available to provide a guide for the conduct of a comprehensive analysis and in turn the development of the comprehensive course of study or training plan.

In the absence of a comprehensive course of study or training plan, the outline may serve, to a limited degree, the needs of an instructor as a basis for presenting his course or training content. It provides at least an outline of content to be covered—the framework. It helps to prevent the instructor from "shooting from the hip."

A course outline, if based on an analysis, is somewhat similar to the instructional schedule which is presented in detail in Chapter 7. The instructional schedule, however, contains the listing of all learning tasks, support materials, aids, and strategies while the course or training outline contains only a listing of the learning tasks in topic form.

Some advantages of a course or training outline include the following:

1. A rather easily prepared document by someone knowledgeable in the field.
2. Provides a quick overview of a course or training plan, provides a review of the "essentials" of the course in easily understood terms.
3. Provides administration with a suitable document which contains essential items necessary for their review and use.
4. Serves as a basis for later course of study and training plan development.

Course/Training Guide

A course guide is very similar in make-up and use as the course outline. As the name implies, it serves as a guide which has been developed by a group or agency from which materials and content can be adapted to local situations. A guide is developed to help provide uniformity of content for a subject area by selected individuals who are considered highly competent in that particular subject area.

An instructor does not teach from a course or training guide. Rather, the instructor uses the guide as a basis for the development of the outline or goes directly to the development of a comprehensive course of study or training plan. A guide when developed by nationally recognized individuals will naturally reflect national thinking and, therefore, have application nationally to that particular subject or training area. However, if it is developed by regional, state or local groups, it will reflect the thinking and have an intended application only for those geographical areas.

The more basic the subject content is, the wider (geographically) the application will be for a developed course or training guide. Figure 2-7, shows the relationship and sequence of the five instructional materials development components.

INSTRUCTIONAL MATERIALS DEVELOPMENT
COMPONENTS SEQUENCE

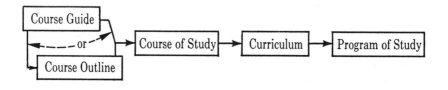

FIGURE 2-7

SUMMARY

The major purpose for planning, organizing and conducting an instructional analysis is to establish the base from which a course of study or training plan can be developed. A number of considerations must be taken into account before adequate instructional materials can be completed. These include, (1) Establishing a philosophy for education and training, (2) Identifying the purposes of selected instructional areas, and (3) Identifying instructional materials development components.

It is imperative that the content analyzer and instructional materials developer recognize and have a philosophy about education and training. Philosophy provides guidelines within which instructional materials are developed. The course and training offerings reflect the institution's as well as the individual instructor's philosophy. It has been found that a number of typical concepts are held by instructors who are learner oriented.

The instructional areas of practical arts, vocational education, industrial education, industrial arts, vocational industrial, and industrial technical education are all part of the career education continuum. These areas provide the broad general emphasis as well as the more specialized vocational emphasis. Career education encompasses all education. Industrial arts, a part of practical arts, has a general orientation and is one of the components of career education. The instructional areas of vocational industrial and industrial technical emphasize the vocational aspects of education providing for the occupational preparation and advancement needs of individuals.

There are five components to be considered in instructional materials development: program of study, curriculum, course of study or training plan, course/training outline, and course/training guide. The course of study or training plan is the one most important to the individual instructor. It is developed from guides and outlines and is a part of a curriculum which, in turn, is a part of the program of study. Each course of study or training plan contains a number of specific components which need to be completed if the instructor is to be adequately prepared to conduct a course or training program.

SUGGESTED QUESTIONS AND ACTIVITIES

1. Prepare a statement of philosophy relating to education and training that you support and one that is acceptable by the institution or agency where you are employed or for whom you plan to work.

2. Observe several industrial educators or trainers for the purpose of identifying their philosophy regarding their offerings. Based on your observation, write a short paper indi-

cating what you think their philosophy is regarding learners, content, and fellow instructors.

3. How do the typical concepts held by industrial instructors differ from concepts held by other instructors? How are they alike?

4. Prepare a graphical presentation of the instructional areas listed in the chapter, including a relationship explanation for use in explaining these areas to advisory groups.

5. Explain why career education is considered a concept rather than a separate educational course or curriculum.

6. After talking with knowledgeable people in the field and reference reading, list the various instructional areas normally included in each of practical arts and vocational education.

7. Justify course offerings, representing the three instructional areas, in a single department of industrial education.

8. List the similarities and differences between industrial arts, vocational industrial, and industrial technical on the points of (1) major purposes, (2) learners served, (3) instructor qualification, and (4) facilities needed.

9. Ask a selected number of supervisors or administrators and instructors in your field for their definition and description of the five instructional materials components listed in the chapter. Compare their answers with your understanding of these terms by developing a one or two page comparison sheet.

10. List five major reasons, in order of priority, why each instructor should have a well developed course of study or training plan.

11. Survey a designated institution or agency for the number of courses of study, training plans or outlines being used by the instructors in your field of interest. Obtain responses from the instructors why they do or do not have and use them.

Part II
Identification
And Selection

chapter 3

Analysis Terminology

E ach discipline or area of study has its own set of terms which, if not completely understood, will cause a lack of understanding of the discipline or area of study and will hinder the accomplishment of the objectives or purposes which have been established. The study of analysis, as it relates to course of study and training plan development, has its own set of terms. When these are once understood and relationships established, the course developer will have a "set-of-tools" necessary to complete an appropriate analysis, which is the basis for a relevant course of study, or training plan.

The development of the inventory of tasks, presented in Chapter 4, can only be accomplished if one has an understanding of analysis terminology. Also, communication with others competent in analysis and course of study or training plan development will be much more effective and productive when the analysis terminology is understood.

This chapter presents and provides an explanation of the essential terminology used in the process of identifying and selecting course or training content. The following topics are presented: (1) Definition and Description of Terms, (2) Duties and Divisions, and (3) Learning Tasks.

CHAPTER OBJECTIVES

Through the study of this chapter and the completion of the suggested questions and activities you will have accomplished the following objectives. You will be able to:

1. Define selected terms used in the conduct of analysis and graphically illustrate their interrelationships.
2. Identify, classify, and correctly state duties and divisions for a particular instructional area.
3. Identify, classify, and correctly state tasks within specific duty and/or division classifications.

DEFINITION AND DESCRIPTION OF TERMS

Terms alone have very little value unless they help communicate understandings and are used in conjunction with the development or conduct of something of interest to the individuals involved. The understanding of each of the following terms is imperative so that the inventory of tasks can be developed and conducted, and a comprehensive analysis be completed in a selected instructional area.

Instructional Analysis

Instructional analysis is a technique or procedure used to more accurately identify the essential content to be included in a designated instructional offering. It is a procedure used to identify important and relevant duties or divisions and their respective learning tasks, which are included in an occupation, a job cluster, a job, an activity, a project, a unit, etc., to be used for a selected instructional situation. The instructional analysis technique is equally effective for both academic and occupational offerings. It may be used as a basis for instructional program development by educational institutions as well as industrial, business, government, and military groups.

Inventory of Tasks

An inventory of tasks is a list of selected and appropriately stated tasks (manipulative, informational, and attitudinal) grouped into categories called major duties or divisons which are normally performed by individuals (workers, student trainees, etc.) in specified occupational or instructional areas.

An inventory of tasks is often referred to as the "task inventory." An inventory of tasks for purposes of instructional content identification and selection is most frequently obtained by following a series of prescribed steps, including research of current literature, completion of specially prepared questionnaires, conducted interviews, and the observation of actual activities being performed.

Duty/Division

A duty or division is a large segment of an occupation, instructional area, a cluster of jobs, a job, or an activity, to be learned by an individual and which contains a number of related tasks. Tasks included in each duty or division may be related on the basis of kind of content, level, and/or complexity. The tasks included in each duty or divison may be manipulative, informational, and/or attitudinal. Duties or divisions, which are somewhat independent of each other, usually contain a minumum of six to twelve related tasks. Duty or division statements are typically stated and include action words ending in "ing."

The term "duty" is usually used when analyzing and developing training programs to meet specific job requirements as found in industry and business training programs. The term "division" is most often used when analyzing and developing courses for use in educational institutions.

The following are examples of duty or division statements:

1. Maintaining and repairing power trains
2. Preparing food
3. Compiling and interpreting data
4. Organizing and planning
5. Training

Task

A task is a discrete learning item having a definite starting and stopping point which can be performed and/or learned within a relatively short period of time. A task may be manipulative (psychomotor), informational (cognitive), or attitudinal (affective). When a task is correctly written, it begins with an action verb and contains a very brief and specific description of what is to be done or known.

Examples of task statements are:

1. Attach stock with specified fasteners
2. File incoming letters
3. Compute cost of materials
4. Follow safety regulations
5. Identify kinds of finishes

A task contains two or more steps (elements) and is a distinct part and is essential for the completion of a job, work activity, or understanding of a large block of informational content. A task involves exerted mental and/or physical effort toward the accomplishment of a predetermined goal.

A task is an action sequence designed to state what the learner is to do, to know or to feel. A task has learning content and, when combined with other appropriate tasks, forms the completion of a project, assignment, problem, or activity.

Task Steps (Subtask or Element)

A listing of very small specific performances or knowledge items when combined in the correct sequence, form a task. Task steps are usually stated in a command form and describe exactly what the learner is to do or know. The task step does not have any value by itself. However, when combined with other appropriate task steps, forms a task which in turn has instructional content value.

The following are examples of task steps (elements):

1. Remove the right pin
2. Avoid touching hot element
3. Record temperature data
4. Turn on switch
5. Return to start

The task step is the smallest unit into which a task can be divided without becoming a simple movement, motion or mental process.

Figure 3-1 illustrates the relationship between the task step, the task, the duty or division, the course, and the subject matter.

RELATIONSHIP OF TERMS

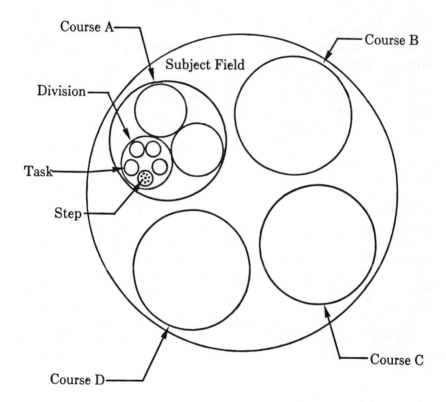

FIGURE 3-1

Job

Although the term *job* has had a number of different meanings in the past, currently, and as accepted by most instructional analysts, it is used to refer to a position or positions held by individuals for which they receive pay. The term payroll job is often used in this instance. A job normally includes duties and tasks which are actually performed by an individual. Job titles are aircraft mechanic, laboratory technician, secondary school mathematics instructor, electrician, etc. A job may be made up of a group of positions which are similar with regard to their duties and respective tasks. The analysis of related jobs is a preliminary step to the development of a task inventory.

In some vocational technical instructional areas, the term job has been used to designate a completed project or activity, or a piece of work completed in the shop or laboratory. To avoid confusion, the term job should be used as it relates to a position held by an individual for which pay is received. Work activities and assignments performed in the course of learning instructional content will be referred to as projects, activities, assignments, or problems.

Position

A position is what an agency or institution has available to be filled by individuals who desire employment in that particular agency or institution. A number of similar positions (with respect to their duties and tasks) make up a job. There are as many positions in any one given agency as might be allocated. A position exists in an agency whether it is filled or not. An analyst usually does not analyze positions, rather, an analysis is made of the job in which similar positions are included.

DUTIES AND DIVISIONS

A duty or a division is a large segment of a course within a proposed instructional area to be learned by an individual, and contains a number of related tasks. These tasks may be related on the basis of kind of content, level, and/or complexity. The use of the term "duty" is used when developing training programs to meet specific job requirements while the term "division" is used primarily when developing courses for educational institutions.

The duties or divisions are usually identified prior to the identification of respective tasks. However, in some cases the opposite may be true, depending upon the available information, the nature of the content, and the expertise of the analyzer.

Almost all jobs and instructional areas can be divided into major identifiable and somewhat independent segments which then become duties or divisions. In some cases a duty or division, if quite large, may become a separate course.

The breaking down of proposed instructional areas into tentative duties or divisions provides for a more orderly and accurate analysis and listing of tasks. This provides an opportunity for the analyzer to concentrate on one duty or division rather than attempting to view the total course area at one time when analyzing for tasks (e.g., concentrating on maintaining power trains rather than the total automotive field; on communicating with employees rather than the overall field of supervision; on assembling procedures rather than on the total field of metal working). For analysis purposes, it is especially beneficial to divide occupational or instructional areas that are comprehensive, complicated and/or complex (e.g., health, metals, management, electronics) into respective duties or divisions.

Identification Criteria

The basis for the identification of duties or divisions does vary from job to job and from one instructional area to another. However, regardless of the number of duties or divisions identified or their titles, as determined by analyzer, a complete and comprehensive analysis will produce the same content (tasks). The meeting of training and education needs rather than production procedures is used as the basis for final selection of duties or divisions. This requires some knowledge about the individuals to be served and how they learn most effectively.

Projects, assignments, and activities do not determine a duty or division. Rather, the content itself (the tasks involved) is the determiner for any major duty or division. Duties or divisions are so selected that students may complete them without direct reference to another duty or division unless a specific prerequisite duty or division has been identified. The size of or the time limit for each duty or division is based upon the content, the student, and the emphasis. A major consideration is that each duty or division must contain related tasks. However, the time required for each duty or division should be such that normal breaks occur for evaluation purposes and that the tasks make up a learning block suitable to meet student needs. Tasks included in the same duty or division are based on previous less complex (level) tasks and exclude the more complex (higher level) tasks which are found in later duties or divisions.

Some specific criteria to consider in selecting duties or divisions for instructional purposes are: (1) Tasks included are related (similar) in content, complexity, or level; (2) The segment of learning is somewhat independent of other segments; (3) They are based on training and educational feasibility rather than productivity; and (4) They are large and important enough to warrant instructional time. In order to more clearly identify a statement as a duty or division, it includes action words ending in "ing," (e.g., performing, maintaining, operating, organizing, etc.).

Duties, as a major training segment for job preparation and divisions as the designated block for educational offerings, can be classified into either people or work related activities. The people related activities which form duties or divisions include managing, supervising, organizing, etc. The work activities include those tasks which involve fabricating, performing, maintaining, repairing, etc.

The selection of duties or divisions is somewhat arbitrary at first so that the analysis can be completed. Following the completion of analysis, the headings are often changed for instructional purposes based on the relationship of tasks to each other, the desired sequence for instructing, and the nature and background of the student.

When identifying duties or divisions for purposes of beginning the analysis and later sequencing, one should ask the following questions, the answers to which will aid in selecting a tentative duty or division:

1. Level of people to be served?
2. Nature of people relationship?
3. Individual responsibility?
4. Tools and equipment to be used?
5. Materials involved?
6. Processes performed?
7. Products produced?
8. Services rendered?
9. Information required?

Duty and Division Statements

Duty and division statements should end in "ing" to help differentiate them from task or goal statements. In most cases an object is used with the "ing" action word.

Some statements commonly found representing duties and divisions (e.g., people and work oriented activities) in job training and educational programs include the following:

1. Maintaining files
2. Organizing and planning training programs
3. Preparing food
4. Maintaining and repairing fuel systems
5. Supervising and implementing
6. Operating calculating equipment
7. Preparing publications
8. Evaluating performance
9. Lubricating procedures
10. Troubleshooting electrical equipment
11. Testing and inspecting
12. Estimating materials
13. Sharpening tools
14. Cleaning and oiling
15. Attaching and assembling
16. Drilling and milling
17. Training
18. Disassembling

Basic Duties and Divisions

It will be found that during the process of analyzing the selected duties or divisions there is a certain segment of content which needs to be presented and learned prior to going any further into the course. This content (the tasks) are usually grouped together and referred to as the introduction section of the course (the basic or core duty/division).

For a duty or division to be considered to be basic or core, certain criteria must be met, which include (1) contain tasks, most of which are prerequisites to tasks included in two or more of the other duties or divisions; (2) tasks included are of the introductory nature—basic; (3) tasks included are themselves related; and (4) tasks tend to be those which lay the groundwork or base for the course (e.g., terminology, approach, rules, safety, etc.).

The basic duty or division is, in most instances, not firmly identified until after the analysis has been completed. After the tasks for a course or training plan have been selected within each of the duties or divisions, each task is reviewed to determine if it should remain in the original duty or division or pulled out and placed in a newly identified duty or division which is introductory in nature.

A major purpose for identifying a basic duty or division is that more effective instruction results since prerequisite skills will have been completed before attempting difficult and complex tasks. By completing a basic unit of content early in the course or session, students may move to a number of different duties or divisions and be assured that they have had the opportunity to complete the prerequisites.

LEARNING TASKS

Tasks are the backbone of the content to be learned. They are discrete learning items which, in most cases, can be learned in a relatively short period of time (within one class period or session or less). Many instructional programs include tasks which represent all three classifications: namely, manipulative, informational and attitudinal. A group of related tasks, based upon their complexity, content, and level, form an appropriate duty or division.

The task may be thought of as an action or informational sequence designed, when combined with other appropriate tasks, to accomplish an objective which may be the completion of a project, assignment, experiment, problem, etc.

A task moves the content under consideration toward the completion of the stated objective. The results of a satisfactorily completed task become the input to the eventual accomplishment of the objective in question. A task, when correctly selected, is one of a series of related tasks (manipulative, informational, or attitudinal) that is needed to complete, produce or further an identifiable output which may be used by itself or actually become a part of something larger.

Identification of Tasks

All learning tasks are classified as either manipulative, informational or attitudinal. The nature and level of the course or training program determines if one, two, or all three of these task classifications are included in the particular course or training program.

The following criteria should be used when reviewing content items for purposes of identifying possible learning tasks.

1. Must be either manipulative, informational, or attitudinal.
2. Is self-contained, independent of others, and is used or performed essentially the same regardless of the assignment or activity in which it is included.
3. It occupies a significant place in the career ladder development process.
4. Has a definite beginning or starting point and an ending or completion point.
5. It must be rateable.
6. It contains learning content which is beyond merely a step in the procedure in performing a skill or obtaining knowledge.
7. Can be identified as a task by individuals who have competencies in the selected area.

8. Must include two or more steps to be performed to complete the task.
9. Is of such length that one or two usually make up a single lesson or session.

Combining Nature of Tasks

More advanced tasks are learned only when beginning and less complex tasks have been accomplished. This is to say that each task, except the very elementary and beginning task, is built on a previous task.

It will be found that when analyzing content for advanced courses or training programs, the task will be selected specifically to meet the needs of that group. If the same content were analyzed for a beginning course, many of the tasks that had been selected for the advanced course would be further divided into small (less complex) tasks designed to fit the beginning or novice student.

This process is referred to as the combining nature of tasks. Some of the tasks selected for beginning students are actually combined to form more complex tasks for advanced students. Actually, tasks identified for beginning courses become steps or sub-tasks within more complex tasks in the advanced courses. The size of the task is only important to the extent that it meets the instructional demands of the students involved, and also that the tasks meet the task identification criteria.

Manipulative Tasks

Manipulative tasks are those in which physical movements are performed and most emphasized. They involve overt activity along with a minimum amount of informational content. The purpose of identifying and teaching manipulative tasks is to cause students to act and perform with proficiency and dexterity. The degree of perfection for each manipulative task depends on the particular situation which is specified through the stated performance objective.

Manipulative tasks involve such activities as cutting, forming, drawing, and assembling. In industrial education these tasks are performed through the use of tools, equipment, and materials. A manipulative task usually deals with the interaction of tools and equipment with selected materials.

Some examples of manipulative tasks include:

1. Drill a hole
2. Apply finish
3. Adjust a carburetor
4. Cut a thread

The depth at which a manipulative task may be taught and learned varies with the level and purpose of the course and the background of and need for it by the student. A student, when first confronted with a manipulative task, perceives it and receives specific instruction on how it is performed. The student then performs the task under careful guidance of the instructor. This is the extent to which a student becomes involved in beginning courses. In more advanced courses the student continues to perform manipulative tasks already learned, along with new ones, and begins to develop an acceptable pattern of performance, resulting in some degree of perfection. Manipulative tasks are usually learned through effective demonstrations given by individuals competent in the area, followed with an application by the student.

Informational Tasks

Informational tasks deal with facts and concepts; the where, when, and why of the content being considered. Informational tasks involve mental activity by the student. It requires the thinking through of problems, as well as the accumulation of factual data.

Competency in informational tasks traditionally has been obtained through formal class sessions. However, much informational content is and should be learned through self-study, individualized instruction and by observation. A very close relationship exists between informational and manipulative tasks in course content areas that include both. Generally, the informational tasks support the manipulative tasks in beginning courses, while the reverse is true in advanced courses and training programs.

There are several levels of informational tasks which are selected on the basis of the student and course objectives. The lowest level deals only with recognition or memorization of facts, which is basic to most all content areas. This, then, would make up a recognizable part of a beginning course. As the learner advances, and as the course and training session become more advanced, the informational tasks involve the comprehension and application of content learned and finally the determination of relationship (analysis and synthesis) and the making of judgments based upon background knowledge learned.

Informational tasks may be further classifed into various categories based on whether they are essential or optional, or they may be classified on the basis of the kind of content regardless whether it is essential or optional. If a scientific approach is used to obtain tasks for a course or training program (use of the inventory of task procedure), it may not be imperative to go into great detail in classifying tasks as the analysis procedure itself will show what kind of tasks and how many and how much is actually needed.

In most instances course and training content does include two major kinds of information, even though it need not be identified as such in the outline. One kind of information is that which is highly technical, including safety as found in manipulative oriented courses, and also that which is the main and essential content of non-manipulative courses. The second kind is information of a general or background nature which is designed to provide a broader understanding of the overall content and its application.

Some examples of informational tasks are:

1. Identify and describe finishes
2. Trace the development of the lathe
3. Check accuracy of forms
4. Compute cost of materials
5. Prepare bids for purchase of equipment

Attitudinal Tasks

Proper attitudes are just as important and often more so in certain courses and training programs than the manipulative and informational content. Attitudes are learned, which means that if relevant attitudes can be identified for a particular course they should be presented so that students will have an opportunity to form the proper attitude whatever it may be. The development of desirable attitudes is essential regardless of the nature and content of a course. Attitudes cause individuals to want or not to want to do certain things. They can facilitate as well as impede learning.

Attitudinal tasks, like manipulative and informational, are quite elementary in beginning courses but become more complex and more difficult to present, learn, and evaluate in advanced courses. The student is usually a passive receiver of stimuli in beginning courses. As the student progresses, the attitudinal task involves responding to a situation, indicating a commitment, and finally changing a behavior system.

Attitudinal tasks are learned by becoming proficient in and involved with manipulative and informational tasks, either formally or informally. These tasks are also learned and behavior changed based on the relationship between a student with other students and with the instructor.

Some examples of attitudinal tasks are:

1. Cooperate in assigned group activity
2. Follow safety precautions
3. Value quality workmanship
4. Greet visitors
5. Show respect for others

Task Statements

In contrast to duty and division statements, tasks are stated in a brief command form using an action verb. The task statement always begins with the action verb and is in terms of the student, stating what the student will do, or what he must know. Among major advantages in stating tasks using an action verb is that they can more easily be converted into performance objectives as the course of study or training plan is being developed.

The task must be stated so that anyone knowledgeable in the field or discipline who reads it will interpret it the same way as the writer. Although the task should be stated briefly, care must be maintained not to omit any key words necessary to accurately describe the intent of the task. For example, if a task is to be performed with a certain tool, the name of the tool needs to be mentioned. If it is obvious which tool will be used, the tool name is omitted.

Some criteria to consider when writing task statements are:

1. Begin with an action verb and include an appropriate object.
2. Write statements in terms recognizable by those competent in the area.
3. Keep statements brief and specific.
4. Use names of tools, equipment, and materials only when absolutely necessary.
5. Do not use words such as use and know as these are not specific enough.
6. State in ratable terms.

Refer to description of manipulative, informational, and attitudinal tasks for examples of task statements that meet the above criteria for stating tasks, presented in previous sections of this chapter.

SUMMARY

The effective use of the analysis technique for the purpose of developing courses of study and training plans requires the understanding of the unique terms involved. Often these terms when used in another context have quite a different meaning. Therefore, it is essential for the analyzer and course developer to have an adequate understanding of the appropriate term.

Instructional analysis is a technique used to identify possible content for course and training program development. An inventory of tasks designed for a selected offering(s) within an instructional area is a result of completing an instructional analysis. Among other considerations for purposes of developing instructional offerings, positions, jobs, job clusters, etc., are analyzed in an effort to identify usable course content, the learning tasks.

Each instructional offering is normally divided into duties or divisions which aid in the initial conduct of a more effective analysis, as well as provide the later structure for the course offering. Duties or divisions are the large segments of a specific offering which contain related tasks—the content to be presented. To avoid confusion with goals, objectives, or task statements, the duties or divisions are usually stated in an "ing" form.

The heart of any instructional offering is the list of learning tasks. Tasks are discrete learning items which in most cases can be performed and/or learned in a relatively short time. Each content item to be classified as a task must meet certain specified criteria. Tasks are of three kinds: manipulative, informational, and attitudinal. A group of related tasks selected on a basis of complexity, content, and level, make up a duty or division. Tasks are stated in a command form using an action verb at the beginning of the statement.

SUGGESTED QUESTIONS AND ACTIVITIES

1. Based upon your study, background, and experience, list a number of reasons for conducting an analysis aside from course or training program development.

2. Write a position paper to be presented to fellow educators stating the value of developing an inventory of tasks prior to instructional material development.

3. Develop a graphical representation, along with a description, showing the relationship of the terms presented in this chapter.

4. Explain the similarities and differences between duties and divisions in a manner that can be readily understood by one not considered to have expertise in the analysis technique.

5. Prepare a brief presentation in which you show and explain what a task is and the nature of the three classifications of tasks.

6. List and justify the criteria you will use for identifying duties or divisions in your instructional area.

7. Explain the nature and purpose of basic duties and divisions.

8. Provide several examples that show the "combining nature" of tasks in each of the manipulative and informational classifications.

9. Correctly state three tasks for a specific course in your instructional area for each of the three classifications.

chapter 4

The Identification of Learning Tasks

To effectively organize, plan, and develop a procedure for identifying learning tasks, one must have an adequate understanding of educational and training philosophy, of the instructional area to be analyzed, of the components that form instructional materials, of the students who will be involved in the proposed course or training program, and of the unique terminology used in the analysis process.

The identification of learning tasks for a selected course or training program make up what is called an inventory of tasks. This inventory of tasks is only one component of the total instructional materials development system. However, it is one of the most important as the further development of instructional materials into courses of study and training plans is dependent upon the completion of this component.

Too often new courses and training programs have been out-of-date and, therefore, not acceptable to the students involved. This has often been due to the use of available textbooks as sole sources or to the limited or narrow educational experiences of those responsible for materials development. At times, traditional content has been accepted without verification and placed within a prescribed time frame without consideration of the amount, type, or kind of content to be included.

The most effective approach for obtaining relevant course content is the development of an inventory of learning tasks based upon a step-by-step procedure which includes feedback from competent individuals and the interpretation of the data in light of the purpose of the course and objectives of the student. This helps to assure obtaining the most relevant content. The development of an inventory of tasks as a major step in instructional materials development has been used effectively by industry, business, and the military. However, this has not always been true in the development of course content by educational institutions.

The use of the inventory procedure for gathering instructional content is a technique that can be followed by any agency whether educational, industrial, business, or governmental. The effective use of the inventory approach requires that individuals be competent in the content area to be analyzed and knowledgeable in the instructional area to be analyzed, or involve those who are. This helps to assure that the content eventually selected will meet the expressed needs of the concerned institution or agency, and the students.

This chapter presents a procedure and the information required for planning, developing, and administering an inventory of tasks in a selected instructional area. The following two topics are treated to help assure the effective use of this technique: (1) Approaches to Task Identification, and (2) Development of the Inventory of Tasks.

CHAPTER OBJECTIVES

Through the study of this chapter and the completion of the suggested questions and activities, you will have accomplished the following objectives. You will be able to:

1. List and describe acceptable task inventory and analysis procedural steps and apply these to a specific situation.
2. Develop a task inventory form for gathering data in a particular instructional area.
3. Develop the procedure and carry out the process of gathering content data (tasks) through the inventory of tasks technique.

APPROACHES TO TASK IDENTIFICATION

The development of a very detailed and comprehensive

course of study or training plan will have little value unless a planned procedure is used to identify content (tasks) designed to meet specified needs. Before the actual course of study or training plan development begins, the content (tasks) needs to be verified, correctly stated, and sequenced.

A number of somewhat ineffective approaches have been used in the past to identify tasks. These include the ivory tower approach where the course developer completes the analysis in the office, making few if any relevant contacts with others. A more desirable procedure has been the charting approach where typical jobs performed in an area are ana- lyzed for tasks, which then form the content base for the in- structional area. This, as is the case in the ivory tower approach, may be extremely biased, especially if only one person completes the analysis. Another format is the use of cards. Here the analyzer writes all of the tasks which have been identified through research and experience on separate cards and then shuffles them to attain suitable instructional sequence.

To be accurate and complete, content for courses and train- ing programs must be gathered from a variety of sources to help assure that they are up-to-date and relevant. Sources from which data might be obtained include research studies, books, completed courses and training plans, questionnaires, interviews, and observations. The role of an analyzer is to make sure the learning tasks identified and the eventual selection is as accurate as possible and that the selected content meets the stated requirements of the course and the needs of the students. The use of the inventory of tasks approach most nearly accomplishes this.

The analyzer must view the proposed instructional setting with the intent and desire to identify specifically what is to be learned. Too frequently only a general idea of what is to be learned is stated. The analysis and study of an instructional area with the objective of describing content in specific terms will help to avoid overlaps as well as fill in voids in the course or training program.

Information gathered which is too general may be useless and that which is too specific and detailed is often too difficult to manage, requiring an excessive amount of time in gathering and tabulating the data.

DEVELOPMENT OF THE INVENTORY OF TASKS

The procedure for the development of an inventory of learning tasks described in this chapter includes twelve essential steps which should be followed if a truly verified body of content is desired for a particular instructional area. The twelve steps, which will be described in detail, are:

1. Identify scope and limitations
2. Review resource materials
3. Develop preliminary duty/division and task list
4. Conduct observations
5. Review by experts
6. Revise inventory
7. Pilot run
8. Finalize revision of inventory
9. Select sample of respondents
10. Administer inventory
11. Record and tabulate data
12. Organize and interpret data

The completion of the twelve steps listed, when carried out in detail, requires considerable time and expense. If time, as well as cost, is a definite obstacle, the procedure can be shortened in several ways. First, which is the least acceptable, is the completion of only steps 1, 2 and 3. This is very close to the ivory tower approach and will tend to emphasize the unwanted bias of the analyzer. It rests heavily on the ability to do research of available materials. A more effective procedure would be to complete steps 1 through 6. In this approach, some feedback through observation and review by experts is built into the analysis procedure. Another procedure would be to complete the first eight steps, which is much more effective than either of the first two abbreviated procedures. In this case, feedback is obtained by not only the experts but also a small representative sample of individuals involved in the instructional area under investigation.

By far the best approach to obtain appropriate duties or divisions and tasks is to follow the twelve steps presented, which helps to provide a verification of the content.

Step 1. Identify Scope and Limitations

First, the major purpose for the educational or training program must be determined. This may be in terms of goals or broadly stated objectives. The program or course may have an occupational, general, or leisure time orientation. It may be designed for specific job preparation, for preparation in a cluster of jobs, for pre-vocational purposes, or for general education reasons. A decision regarding the overall purpose is necessary before going on to the eventual development of the data gathering instrument. If the scope is too large, a great amount of wasted time will be used to gather data which is not essential.

The need for the course or training program and, in turn, the collection of data must also be established. The procedure should be initiated only if the proposed offering meets the needs of interested individuals, if employment opportunities are available, if possibilities of transfer or for credit are available, and if other agencies or institutions are not already providing such courses or programs.

Step 2. Review Resource Materials

For most curriculums, courses, or programs, some initial analysis work has already been completed. The analyses may be in various forms including completed research studies, technical textbooks, workshop reports, individual instructor courses of study, classroom assignments, job descriptions and specifications, national, state and district curriculums, and course or training guides or outlines.

Various publications from professional organizations, such as those of the American Vocational Association, American Industrial Arts Association, American Society for Training and Development, National Association of Industrial and Technical Educators, and the American Association of Community and Junior Colleges should be reviewed for sources of analyses. Various research groups, agencies or associations should be contacted, especially those within the particular state or region. One such agency is the State Research Coordinating Unit which is concerned with the total vocational and technical field. This Unit is usually located in the State Department of Education or in one of the state's universities.

Step 3. Develop Preliminary Duty/Division and Task List

Following the identification of the major purpose of the proposed course or training program and the review of available resource materials, the development of a preliminary list of duties or divisions and tasks is begun. The preliminary listing of tasks must be broader or more comprehensive than the final expected result, to be sure that all tasks will be included. This means that all levels of a job, job cluster, instructional area, etc., which include similar tasks, are to be included unless this becomes too comprehensive and cumbersome to handle through the proposed interview or questionnaire. For example, it is recommended that when developing a course in the metals area, tasks be identified that may be required prior to the proposed course as well as beyond. Also, when developing instructional materials for supervisory training, tasks representing the continuum of supervision should be included. From the tasks obtained in this manner, the eventual course(s) will be identified based on respondent's replies.

There is no precise way used to determine the exact number of duties or divisions and tasks to be included in the inventory form. A limiting factor, however, is the background and interest of the selected respondents and their willingness and ability to respond to a questionnaire. Normally, the longer the inventory the less chance of a high return. However, this does depend upon the interest and commitment that the respondents may have. An in-plant group (captive group) will, in most cases, respond in greater numbers than if the respondents have very little attachment to the individual or the agency administering the inventory.

First, the tentative duties or divisions must be identified following the criteria and procedure in Chapter 3. These are tentative at this time, being used mainly to categorize and help group the tentative list of tasks. Often the duty or division statements are restated, combined, or deleted, following the completion of the gathering of data based on respondents' replies. Each duty or division statement must contain a set of related tasks. Following the development of categories (duties /divisions), the task statements are listed under the respective headings. Each task must meet the criteria described in Chapter 3 to be considered and included in the inventory of tasks.

In the process of reviewing completed analyses, job descriptions, etc., for the purpose of obtaining a tentative list of duties or divisions and tasks, a number of preliminary approaches or formats may be used which are effective to the extent that they fit the sources available and the nature of the content under study. Three formats considered are: (1) Outline Format, (2) Project Analysis Format, and (3) Space Relationship Format.

Outline Format. This format is the traditional type and is similar in use to normal outlining procedures. The course or program is first identified. Then the name of the duty or division is listed, followed by a listing of tasks included in that duty or division. The tasks are listed in an instructional sequence where possible, indicating whether they are manipulative, informational or attitudinal.

This format is used when a considerable number of previously completed analyses and other sources of duties or divisions and tasks are already available. In the initial draft, usually only one duty or division is placed on each page. The outline format is quite similar to the final inventory of tasks form, which is used as the questionnaire or as the interview form, to obtain responses to the task listings. Figure 4-1 is an example of a partially completed Outline Format.

Analysis Chart Format. The analysis chart format is often used when an analysis is based primarily on the projects or products produced within a certain content area. This format is most appropriate in areas of instruction which have a heavy emphasis on manipulative content. It is also useful when checking to see if an existing analysis is complete by identifying typical projects produced, analyzing each, then checking if all tasks have been included. Figure 4-2 is an example of a partially completed Project Analysis Format. When using this format, the project name is usually placed at the top of the page and the respective tasks listed along the side. The checking of each task below the appropriate project provides a tentative sequencing of the tasks. Those tasks having the most check marks along the horizontal row are retained and the ones with the greatest frequency of check marks are taught first.

Space Relationship Format. The space relationship format is used to gather preliminary duties or divisions and tasks in areas where there is a lack of existing completed analyses or prepared course materials. It is most effectively used when tasks must be identified from job descriptions, through obser-

OUTLINE FORMAT
Task Listing Form

Course/Training Program___Beginning Drafting_____

Major Duty/Division____Introduction_____ No.___1_____

Analyst____Paul Henry_____ Date Developed_11-75_

No.	TASK DESCRIPTION	CLASSIFICATION		
		Manip.	Infor.	Attit.
1	Value importance of drafting			X
2	Identify kinds of paper		X	
3	Explain uses of drawing pencils		X	
4	Attach paper to board	X		
5	Sharpen pencils	X		
6	Measure with scales		X	
7	List and explain line weights		X	
8	Draw vertical lines	X		
9	Draw horizontal lines	X		
10	Draw arcs and circles	X		
11	Observe quality standards			X
12	List drafting occupations		X	
13				
14				
15				
16				
17				
18				
19				

FIGURE 4-1

vation techniques, or based upon the background of the analyzer. A major advantage of this approach is that the total
tentative instructional program, course, or plan appears on

one page, showing relationships and also omissions and over-laps. It is most flexible and provides a simplified approach in obtaining a tentative list of duty or division and task statements.

ANALYSIS CHART FORMAT

PROJECTS/PRODUCTS

Task Listing Form

COURSE/TRAINING PROGRAM___Woods___

TASK DESCRIPTION	1 Cutting Board	2 Tray	3 Book Rack	4 Lamp	5 Chair	6 Chest	7 Desk	8	9
1 Measure stock	x	x	x	x	x	x	x		
2 Cross cut stock	x	x	x	x	x	x	x		
3 Rip cut stock	x	x	x	x	x	x	x		
4 Plane surface	x	x	x		x	x	x		
5 Plane edge	x	x	x		x	x	x		
6 Plane end	x		x		x	x	x		
7 Bore hole		x	x	x			x		
8 Shape edge		x	x		x		x		
9 Saw curves			x				x		
10 Prepare surface for finishing	x	x	x	x	x	x	x		
11 Attach with screws		x	x		x		x		
12 Cut dado joints						x	x		
13 Apply lacquer						x	x		
14									
15									
16									
17									
18									
19									
20									

FIGURE 4-2

The name of the proposed course, training program, job, job cluster, instructional area, occupation, etc., is placed in the center circle. Circles, which represent the duties or divisions of the course or training program, are placed so that they overlap the center circle. Extending from each overlapping circle is a list of tasks which have been tentatively identified. The tasks may or may not be identified as manipulative, informational, or attitudinal at this point. Figure 4-3 is an example of a partially completed Space Relationship Format.

Step 4. Conduct Observations

As soon as a preliminary list of duties or divisions and tasks have been identified through the study of available sources and with the use of one or more of the three approaches described in Step 3, appropriate observation procedures should be set up. In some instances the observations of individuals who are involved in the areas to be analyzed will not be practical or possible. However, a concerted effort should be made to actually observe persons working and performing in the area(s) being analyzed. Changes can more easily be made during the actual observations if the tasks are grouped under the appropriate duty or division statements using the outline format.

Observations should be conducted involving a number of different people engaged in employment at various locations. This will help to prevent any bias that might develop. On the basis of these observations, changes should be made and the inventory data revised and again listed in outline form with each duty or division beginning on a new page.

Step 5. Review by Experts

As soon as the tentative inventory has been developed from available sources and updated through observations, it should be reviewed by other individuals who are knowledgeable in the field. The purpose of this step is to help to refine the statements, eliminate obvious misstatements and fill in voids. Knowledgeable individuals will help to make the inventory more relevant and assure that it will be understood by the respondents at a later date.

SPACE RELATIONSHIP
Analysis Form

<u>CLEANING</u>

(M) Wash floors
(M) Wax floors
 (I)   Identify kinds of wax
(M) Clean table tops
(M) Wash windows
(A) Value quality of work
(A) Dress appropriately
 (I)   Describe characteristics
       of cleaners
(M) Vacuum carpets

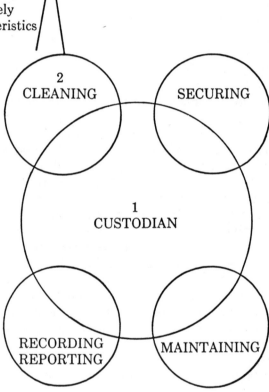

<u>LEGEND</u>

1 - Course or Training Plan Title
2 - Major Duty or Division
3 - Specific Tasks
     M - Manipulative
     I - Informational
     A - Attitudinal

FIGURE 4-3

Experts are selected on the basis of their competence, practical experience, and their interest in the instructional program to be developed. Their selection should represent various levels, differing employment positions, and a sample of employing agencies. The review by experts is usually conducted through the use of an interview. In some cases this may not be possible. In this event, the tentative task inventory, along with an adequate explanation, should be provided to the selected experts. It must be emphasized that the expert must understand the purpose of the inventory and the nature of the proposed course or training program. Each duty or division and respective task should be reviewed critically for such items as clarity, specificity, placement, and necessity.

Step 6. Revise Inventory

Based upon the results of observation and the feedback from the experts, the total inventory is reviewed and revised in preparation for the pilot run. Changes are noted and a revised inventory is assembled. It is desirable to have the same individual revise the inventory who initially developed it and who consulted with the experts. All statements are to follow the criteria established for duties or divisions and tasks. An attempt should be made to group related tasks within a duty or division. Also, in some cases tasks may be listed in a tentative sequence reflecting learning theory and/or the order of performance.

The tasks making up the inventory should be organized into a suitable format and duplicated for easy reading. The tentative format should not only contain the duty or division and task statements, but also the tentative directions for the respondents, a rating scale for evaluating individual tasks as to need, importance, etc., and a cover sheet requesting general background information of each respondent. Figure 4-4 is an example of a Background Information format. This should be adapted to fit the particular need and situation to obtain information relative to the instructional area being analyzed.

A suggested format for the listing and rating of the tasks is presented in Figure 4-5. The general instructions, as well as the rating categories, will change based upon the purposes and content being analyzed. Of great importance is the scale to which the respondents will react in rating the specific

BACKGROUND INFORMATION

CHECK THE TYPE OF CLUSTER (OR COURSES) IN WHICH YOU PROVIDE INSTRUCTION.

_____ Automotive   _____ Building Trades
_____ Welding   _____ Data Processing
_____ Culinary Arts   _____ Electrical
_____ Air Conditioning   _____ Radio and TV Repair
_____ Clerical   _____ Heavy Equipment
_____ Meat Cutting   _____ Health Occupations
_____ Cashier Sales   _____ Maintenance Mechanics
_____ Auto Body   _____ Diesel Mechanics
_____ Machinist   _____ Pre-Vocation Orientation
_____ Hospitality   _____ Other
_____ Basic Related Education

CHECK FULL-TIME INSTRUCTIONAL EXPERIENCE.

__ (1) Began this year   __ (4) Have taught three to five years
__ (2) Have taught one year   __ (5) Have taught five to ten years
__ (3) Have taught two years   __ (6) Have taught over ten years

---

CHECK INSTRUCTOR TRAINING AND/OR COLLEGE DEGREES YOU HAVE COMPLETED AND COMPLETE BLANKS.

_____ (1) Instructor training workshops and seminars (non-credit)
_____ (2) Instructor training workshops and seminars (credit)
_____ (3) Type of certificates held_____
_____ (4) Associate Degree: Major_____
_____ (5) Bachelor's Degree: Major_____
_____ (6) Above Bachelor's Degree: Major_____

FIGURE 4-4

INSTRUCTIONS FOR COMPLETING THE INSTRUCTOR COMPETENCY INVENTORY

Carefully read each of the competency statements listed below and on the following pages. Then rate each one which you think Skill Center instructors should be able to perform and have knowledge of to be considered effective instructors.

Rate each competency statement by placing a number 1, 2, 3, 4, or 5 in the column labeled "Importance & Use" which most clearly estimates the importance and use of the instructor competency in relationship to the total list of competencies in that section.

At the end of each section, in the space provided, write in and rate any additional tasks which you think Skill Center instructors should be able to perform, have competency in, and knowledge of:

SKILL CENTER INSTRUCTOR COMPETENCY INVENTORY

Listed below are six major sections and a list of specific instructor competencies under each. Rate each competency which you think Skill Center instructors should be able to perform and have knowledge of. Add additional competencies which are not listed, then rate the ones you have listed.	IMPORTANCE & USE 1. Not important. 2. Below average in importance. 3. Average in importance. 4. Above average in importance. 5. Highly important.

SECTION I. ORIENTATION AND INTRODUCTION

	COMPETENCY STATEMENTS	
No.	Skill Center instructors should be able to:	
1.	Have knowledge of the purposes and policies of the Skill Center.	
2.	Maintain appropriate trainee and facility records.	
3.	Maintain appropriate financial accounts.	
4.	Prepare and submit required reports.	
5.	Understand certification requirements for occupational instructors.	
6.	Compare community college skill center occupational education and industry/business training programs.	
7.	Understand occupational education terminology.	
8.	Identify responsibilities of Skill Center instructors.	
9.	List and explain qualities of effective instructors.	

FIGURE 4-5

tasks. Their reactions will ultimately determine tasks to be included, as well as their sequence for training and education programs. It must be remembered that the longer the list and the greater number of responses required, the fewer returns will be received and, in many instances will be less valid.

Two basic responses are required concerning the rating of each task listed: (1) Is it a required task, and (2) How important is the task in relationship to others. In some cases, time spent is substituted for (2) above, and whether the respondent performs the task for (1) above. Usually a 3, 5, or 7 point scale is used to indicate the importance of or time spent in performing a particular task. In most cases a five point scale will provide adequate data. The levels, using importance and time spent, might be as follows:

Importance	Time Spent
5 - highly important	5 - most of the time
4 - very important	4 - considerable time
3 - important	3 - some time
2 - somewhat important	2 - very little time
1 - not important	1 - no time

Step 7. Pilot Run

Prior to the actual administration of the task inventory, it should be tested to help identify any discrepancies it may contain. At this point it is essential to get some input from a selected few respondents with regard to the clarity and understanding of the duty or division and task statements. Also, it is important to have the directions reviewed for understandability.

Selected respondents during the pilot run should respond to the total inventory, including the rating of each of the tasks so that suggestions may be received for use in revising the inventory. The selection of the individuals who form the pilot group should be representative of the sample to be used later in the final administration of the inventory. As a result of the pilot run, the following should be obtained.

1. Suggestions for revising the general information sheet.

2. More clearly stated duty or division and task statements.
3. Deletion of irrelevant tasks.
4. Addition of omitted tasks.
5. Reaction to proposed rating system.
6. Clarification of directions used for those completing the inventory.
7. An estimation of time used in completing the inventory.
8. Suggestions with regard to overall format.

Step 8. Final Revision of Inventory

The major purpose of the final revision step is to carry out a final check on all parts of the inventory format. The results from the pilot run, as well as comments and suggestions made by the experts, are reviewed and incorporated in the final inventory form to make it more effective. Each duty or division and task statement should be checked for clarity and specificity so that the interpretation will be the same by all. It is also critical that the proposed rating scale fits the content and is easily understood.

As soon as a final draft of the inventory is agreed upon, the material should be duplicated, using a process which will have a professional appearance. A quantity of inventory materials sufficient for second mailings should be produced, as well as extra copies for use in discussing the project and for final reports. Another important item to consider and complete at this time is the development of a tabulation chart to fit the inventory responses. Quite often the tabulation will be done by hand. However, if data processing equipment is available the analyzer should contact knowledgeable persons to check the inventory with regard to its appropriateness for machine tabulation.

Step 9. Select Sample Respondents

Unless the prospective respondents have been appropriately selected to represent a cross section of knowledgeable individuals, the efforts in completing the previous steps in detail will have been wasted. A major and most important part of the procedure in developing and administering the task inventory is surveying a sample of individuals who can provide the verification of selected duties or divisions and tasks. Regardless of individuals, groups, or agencies available, the important thing is that the prospective respondents are representative of the population, including the graduates of a similar offering, and those who will be trained in the particular content under investigation.

It is often desirable to contact associations, institutions, organizations, societies, unions, industries, businesses, or other groups which include individuals who represent the training content under consideration. In some cases the individuals may be selected directly without going through an association, agency, etc. Probably the most accepted approach is to request lists of recommended names to whom the inventory can be sent. If the course to be developed is of general orientation, a sample from a total area population may be drawn using appropriate sampling techniques. The size of the sample depends upon a number of factors such as uniqueness of the proposed course, available respondents, and time and money available.

Step 10. Administer the Inventory

A major concern at this point is the possibility of an adequate return from the questionnaires mailed out. Some suggestions to more effectively accomplish an adequate return include:

1. Have all materials duplicated using the same process and done in a professional manner.
2. Provide a self-addressed and stamped envelope.
3. Include a cover letter written by one(s) who commands respects of respondents and others.
4. Provide needed examples of what is to be done.
5. Assemble materials so that they are easily understood and responses can be made quickly.
6. Develop a mailing chart, including a numbering system, so that a record can be kept of materials sent out and returned.

7. Be sure all directions are brief and specific.
8. Provide some incentives which may be in a form of an appeal to respondents, or of a monetary nature.

Follow-up letters and additional questionnaires need to be provided. As in most cases, the first mailing very seldom provides sufficient returns for adequate verification of tasks.

One must be sure that all necessary materials are included when the inventory is mailed to prospective respondents. The following items should be included:

1. A cover letter which indicates the purpose and provides the motivation, signed by an individual or representative of a group, agency, etc., who enjoys the respect of the respondents.
2. The inventory, with appropriate instructions and examples, listing the duties or divisions and tasks, and an appropriate rating scale.
3. A self-addressed and stamped return envelope.

In some instances the inventory is administered directly by the analyzer, being handed directly to the respondent or used as an interview form. As when mailing the inventory, a representative sample must be used to help assure verified results. Care should be taken in either approach that lines of communications are followed when sending or personally administering the inventory. A greater acceptance and response always occurs if support is obtained by the respective individuals in charge. These individuals can help to motivate and promote the completion of the inventory by those who are under their supervision.

Step 11. Record and Tabulate Data

It is important that the same individual who developed the inventory also be the one to either perform or be in charge of the recording and the tabulation of the data from the returned inventories. If data processing is used, the data will be automatically recorded according to the input information given. If the data is to be recorded by hand, a blank inventory form may be used or a special form prepared so that tabulation can be made based on categories of responding individual's backgrounds. Whether machine or hand tabulated, data for each task may be recorded and later compared on the basis of years of employment or experience, years of education, age of respondents, employment position, or etc. When recording data in this way, content for instructional programs (courses, training program, etc.) can be more nearly tailored to the needs of specific groups who will be participants of the particular offering.

Step 12. Organize and Interpret Data

Care must be taken so that the inventory is initially developed and finally tabulated to provide information which is truly useful for course or training program development. When data have been collected based on respondents according to various categories as described in Step 11, the needs of specific groups can more nearly be met. Also, multilevel educational or training programs may be more accurately developed, providing for a career ladder approach. Responses by more experienced respondents would be considered for more advanced offerings while responses from beginning respondents might make up the large portion of initial courses. If the rating scale for each task is based on most important to not important, or great amount of time to little time involved, an interpretation will need to be made by the analyzer as to its inclusion and at what level. Also, decisions need to be made as to whether the task is best learned on-the-job or in a more formal instructional setting. Chapter 5 will treat in more detail the process to follow in selecting and the sequencing of tasks, which is an extension of Step 12.

SUMMARY

Effective courses of study and training programs are based upon content (tasks) which has been selected following an identification procedure which includes a verification process. Too often in the past instructional content has been selected based only on available reference materials, or on a single person's background and experience. The most effective approach to obtain relevant content is the development of an inventory of tasks from which specific tasks are selected for proposed courses or training programs. This approach is applicable to any subject matter field and level.

The development of an inventory of tasks includes twelve steps if a truly verified body of content is desired. These steps include the following:

1. Identify scope and limitations
2. Review resource materials
3. Develop preliminary duty/division and task list
4. Conduct observations
5. Review by experts
6. Revise inventory
7. Pilot run
8. Finalize revision of inventory
9. Select sample of respondents
10. Administer inventory
11. Record and tabulate data
12. Organize and interpret data

The twelve steps may need to be modified to fit a particular situation or imposed limitations. However, any great change in the steps, including the elimination of some, may reduce the validity of the content eventually selected for a particular course or training program. Of special significance in the development of the inventory of tasks is the involvement of as many knowledgeable individuals as possible to help assure obtaining up-to-date data which are later transformed into instructional content. Where possible, the responsibility of developing and administering the inventory of tasks should rest with one individual to provide for continuity and uniformity.

The formats developed and used must fit the content to be identified and selected. It must also be so designed and expressed in language to match the respondents' education and experience so that the greatest value and results may be obtained. The final interpretation of data for use in the later development of courses of study and training plans is effective only to the extent that the proper procedure was followed and the appropriately designed gathering instruments were used.

SUGGESTED QUESTIONS AND ACTIVITIES

1. Present a list of reasons why an inventory of tasks should be developed prior to the preparation of course materials.

2. Complete the following for each of the twelve steps in developing an inventory of tasks:

   a. Major reasons for carrying out the step in detail.
   b. What will be the effect if that particular step is not completed?
   c. What adaptation of the step will you need to make in your situation?
   d. Calculate the cost involved in manpower and materials.

3. Identify several courses or training programs in which you have been involved, either as presenter or participant. For each of these identify the specific steps (of the twelve) that were followed in the preparation of the content. In what ways could each of the courses or training programs have been improved?

4. Develop a task inventory format, and related documents, designed to obtain verified content for a particular instructional area. Indicate the instructional area and its level and purpose. This is to include:

   a. General Information Form
   b. Inventory of Tasks Form
   c. Tabulation Form

5. Identify a tentative list of duties or divisions and tasks, using acceptable procedures. Compile such a list placing it in an inventory of tasks format for use in obtaining responses from representative individuals knowledgeable in the field.

6. Develop and carry out a step-by-step procedure in gathering content data (tasks) for a selected instructional area using the inventory of tasks technique. Include a time line and the estimated cost.

chapter 5

Task Selection, Sequencing, and Detailing

The selection of learning tasks, their eventual sequencing for learning efficiency, and the detailing of these tasks form the basis for the development of educational courses and training programs. The initial selection of the tasks is done without regard to the existing limitations, such as lack of facilities, personnel, time, and funds. Modification of the content selected, because of these and other limitations, is made to fit specific situations as they arise.

The conduct of an appropriately developed inventory of tasks questionnaire or interview form will assure obtaining a suitable list of learning tasks. If developed and carried out according to the suggested steps, a greater number of tasks will have been identified and rated than could possibly be included in any one course or training program. This is done to make sure that no omissions occur and also that tasks will be identified for those who need to gain pre-requisite competency, as well as those who may progress more rapidly and desire to go beyond the minimum requirements of the particular offering.

The data obtained through responses to the task inventory need to be recorded, organized, and interpreted so that the selection of appropriate tasks for a specific offering can be made. Following this, the selected duties or divisions and tasks are sequenced, after which each task is detailed so that the instructional content may be presented and learned more effectively.

A number of approaches are presented in this chapter to more effectively solve the problem of selecting, sequencing, and detailing relevant learning tasks. The following topics are presented to accomplish this phase of course of study or training plan development: (1) Tabulation and Interpretation of Inventory Data, (2) Selection Criteria and Procedures, (3) Sequencing Criteria and Procedures, and (4) Task Detailing.

CHAPTER OBJECTIVES

Through the study of this chapter and the completion of the suggested questions and activities, you will have accomplished the following objectives. You will be able to:

1. Tabulate and interpret data received from the inventory of tasks for use in selected courses of study or training plans.
2. Select learning tasks for a course or training program based upon stated criteria using acceptable procedures and formats.
3. Sequence selected tasks within duties or divisions to be included in a particular offering, following stated criteria and using appropriate procedures and formats.
4. Using an approved format, detail selected manipulative and informational tasks, following stated steps of procedure.

TABULATION AND INTERPRETATION OF INVENTORY DATA

For most accurate results, the individual who developed the inventory should be the one who interprets and evaluates the responses received. If this is not possible, the same individual should at least be involved in the total process and preferably be responsible for the entire process. Regardless of how carefully the inventory has been developed, certain decisions will need to be made when the data is obtained. These include the specificity and levels, as well as questions concerning the meeting of stated criteria. If one person has this responsibility, a greater chance of uniformity and accuracy will occur.

The accurate interpreting and evaluating of inventory data is most valuable and essential to the later developing of instructional materials. One must be sure that the returns were recorded and a follow-up of non-returns made so that the eventual data represents a cross section of responses appropriate to the particular area under study.

Tabulating Data

The inventory should be developed in such a manner as to permit the use of data processing procedures if these facilities as well as funds are available. All input data must be verified to be sure that the output data is accurate. In many cases there are limited funds as well as limited access to data processing facilities, which then requires that the tabulation of data be done by hand.

The tabulating of data and its interpretation also depend upon the information obtained through the background information sheet completed by each respondent. Tasks for certain offerings are selected based upon the responses of those who reside in a certain location, number of years of experience, years of education, ages, etc. In this way offerings can be developed for such groups as beginning students or novices, advanced students, and local area residents. This permits a course or training program to be developed which more nearly meets stated needs and objectives.

Regardless of whether tabulating is done by machine or hand, an acceptable procedure needs to be followed so that the tabulated data can be interpreted and evaluated for inclusion in specific courses or training programs. The method of tabulation is based upon the questions asked on the background information form and the rating scales used in the inventory. Quite often the arithmetic mean is used to summarize the data collected regardless of the basis of the rating (e.g., time, importance, etc.). The analyzer merely sums up all the responses for each task and divides by the number of respondents, thus obtaining the mean value for that particular task. Different mean values will usually be obtained when comparing responses by different groups as identified from the background information form.

Interpreting Data

Following the tabulation of responses to the tasks in the inventory, the analyzer is ready to begin the interpretation of the data in light of the specific course(s) to be developed.

If the arithmetic mean has been used to summarize the responses, some decision needs to be made regarding at what point the mean value is too low or is high enough so that the particular task in question may be deleted or retained. Often an arbitrary decision is made at this point, using the consideration of time, importance, complexity, etc., as a basis.

In some instances a 50% response level is used. Some prefer to follow the practice of technical and governmental agencies of using a 70% cut-off point as is followed in accepting or rejecting applicants for positions. If a rating scale of 1 to 5 was used, all tasks that have a 2.5 or 3.0 value may be retained depending upon the particular situation. There is no absolute right or wrong way for making this determination. Justification can be presented for about any level used as a cut-off point depending upon such factors as nature of content, time allowable, competence desired, etc. For instance, a time limitation will cause the analyzer to select a higher mean value in most instances.

The following is an example of a table set-up using *importance* and a 3.00 as the retention cut-off point for all of the tasks included in the inventory.

	Task No.	Mean Rating	Retain
Duty A	1	2.96	
	2	3.01	x
	3	4.21	x
	4	3.36	x
	•		
	•		
Duty B	1	3.57	x
	2	2.05	
	3	1.97	
	4	3.26	x
	•		
	•		

If it is found that too many tasks are retained using 3.00, a higher cut-off point may be selected. If a number of different ratings are used, such as importance and time spent, ratings of both will need to be considered in determining the specific task to retain. In most cases a decision will need to be made which rating takes precedence if there is a conflict in the ratings of a particular task.

Respondents may have added some tasks to the returned task inventory. If this does occur, the tasks should be carefully reviewed and evaluated as to possible inclusion in the proposed course or training program. Before including these tasks, each must be reviewed by experts and hopefully reacted to by a selected sample of respondents.

SELECTION CRITERIA AND PROCEDURES

A major problem facing course developers is that two individuals often do not see particular tasks and the resulting objectives in the same way. One may see a task as highly important, or complex, or time consuming, while another individual may look at it quite differently. This may be due to a number of factors, one of which is the competency level of the individuals concerned. The mere fact of being aware of this problem helps to attain a more relevant offering. This possible inconsistency does cause one to question the value of courses of study and training plans that have been developed in the past.

Before any kind of procedure is placed into practice regarding the specific selection of tasks for a particular offering, it is essential that the initial gathering of data (the appropriate development of a tentative inventory of tasks and critical feedback by respondents) has been carried out effectively. It is only after a comprehensive inventory of tasks has been obtained and tabulated that decisions can be made regarding the selection of specific tasks to meet specific situations.

In the selection of tasks, the basic question is which ones should be included and which excluded. In order to do this effectively, some criteria and/or plan must be devised which will fit the particular situation. The course developer must remember that accurate selection of tasks provides the most powerful justification for the requested resources required to provide the education and training. The identification and selection of resources under ideal situations, however, does not come about until after the content has been identified and selected based upon some organized set of procedural steps.

Realistically, limitations such as lack of facilities, time, funds, etc., must be recognized and considered. However, this should be done after the instructional content for a selected offering has been identified. This will help to assure that the content will be relevant and will meet the needs as specified prior to the development of the inventory of tasks.

Selection Criteria

Responses to the initial task inventory provide the basic criteria that must be considered when selecting tasks for courses and training programs. Additional criteria must also be considered when selecting the initial list of tasks for a particular offering.

Tasks to be considered for a specific course or training program should meet a selected number of the following criteria:

1. *Frequency of performance and use.* Tasks which are frequently performed and used by most of those in the instructional area should be selected for inclusion in the course or training program
2. *Importance and need.* These tasks are oft-considered essential to the accomplishment of the overall content regardless of whether they might be frequently used or performed. Also tasks involving safety and health are considered highly important, yet they are often not frequently used or performed.
3. *Basic and required.* Tasks which form the prerequisites for later learning need to be selected even though they might fit better in another course or learned more effectively on-the-job. This also includes those tasks considered to be common to many other related tasks.
4. *Complexity and difficulty.* Only those tasks which

can be effectively learned by the anticipated students should be included. In some cases highly complex and difficult tasks should be delayed until students become more mature and competent. However, if a task is highly complex as well as being considered difficult, this does not mean that it should be excluded on this criterion alone. If it is critical and essential before other learning can take place within the specific course, it must be included.

5. *Immediacy.* A number of tasks, depending upon the specific course or training program, are needed just prior to employment or the next course. These will need to be included regardless of whether they meet some of the other criteria (e.g., writing resumes, etc.).

6. *Time element.* Although this is considered as one of the limitations, it can be referred to at the time of initial selection. If it is known that a certain segment of time has been allotted, tasks requiring a great amount of time for competence might be eliminated or reduced to a number of smaller tasks, retaining only those which meet the other criteria.

7. *Appropriateness for setting.* Even though a number of tasks may meet most of the other criteria, certain ones may not be appropriate or efficiently learned during a class or laboratory session. Many tasks may be more effectively taught and learned on the job.

8. *Duplication.* Prior courses and training programs should be reviewed for tasks included to avoid over duplication of instructional effort. Some repetition is essential for effective learning. However, gross duplication must be avoided.

9. *Meet task statement criteria.* Even though the tasks were initially identified based on whether they met the specified criteria, it is important to review them again. It may be that certain tasks may no longer meet the criteria as applied to a selected course due to background of learners, level of course, etc.

The above listed criteria are not necessarily all inclusive. Rather, they represent the major considerations about which educators and trainers hopefully have some degree of control. Each task should be selected on a basis of its evaluation against each of the criteria before a final decision is made.

Selection Procedure

Some form of charting may be developed and used to assist in the selection of essential learning tasks for a particular course or training program. Two of these approaches are the Analysis Chart Format and the Outline Format. These are used in addition to the information obtained through the inventory questionnaire.

Analysis Chart Format. The analysis chart makes use of typical projects produced or activities performed in an instructional area. These are placed at the top of the chart with the tasks listed in the left hand column. As each project or activity is analyzed, the tasks contained are listed and checked below the appropriate project or activity. Those tasks containing the greatest number of check marks are retained since they are the ones considered most important and, in turn, most frequently used.

This approach is very effective if the content area has a heavy manipulative emphasis. However, care must be taken not to forget to include the information and attitudinal tasks. These will not be as easily detected as will the manipulative tasks when using this approach. Figure 5-1 similar to Figure 4-2, shows the analysis chart format which may be used for task selection.

Outline Format. An approach which has a much broader application is the outline format. This format can easily and effectively be used in all instructional areas regardless of whether they are classroom or laboratory oriented. The outline format includes a listing of identified tasks within respective duties or divisions. Columns are provided so that each task can be evaluated against selected criteria items which, in turn, provide a numerical rating. The ratings are assigned quantitative values, with those tasks having the highest rating being considered as relevant for the particular course. Figure 5-2 shows the outline format and some typical rating items often used.

ANALYSIS CHART FORMAT

Task Selecting Form   PROJECTS/PRODUCTS

COURSE/TRAINING PROGRAM _____

TASK DESCRIPTION

	1	2	3	4	5	6	7	8	9
1									
2									
3									
4									
5									
6									
7									
8									
9									
10									
11									
12									
13									
14									
15									
16									
17									
18									
19									
20									

FIGURE 5-1

An ideal listing of tasks will be developed as a result of evaluating each task against the stated criteria. Only at this point should such limitation factors as available funds, space, equipment, etc., be considered. The various limitations usually further reduce the list of tasks. Often tasks which might

TASK SELECTION

Outline Format

Course/Training Programs _____

Major Duty/Division _____ No. _____

Analyst _____ Date _____

NO.	TASK DESCRIPTION	Rating 5 (High) 4, 3, 2, 1 (Low)					
		Freq.	Imp.	Basic	Comp.	Imm.	Time
1							
2							
3							
4							
5							
6							
7							
8							
9							
10							
11							
12							
13							
14							
15							

Legend

   Freq. - Frequency of use

   Imp. - Importance and need

   Basic - Basic and required

   Comp.- Complexity and difficulty

   Imm. - Immediacy of use

   Time - Time allotment

FIGURE 5-2

effectively be taught in a more formal setting are left to on-the-job instruction due to various additional limitation factors.

Tasks for selected offerings may be either optional or required. This must also be considered when making task selections. Another limitation is the wide and varying background of students who are enrolled in the particular offering. The amount of time allowed for a course is another factor which enters into the selection process and one which may change from one year to another, and from one agency to another. To provide greater flexibility to meet these various needs and demands, additional tasks may be included which are optional in nature for most of the students, but will fill a specific need for those with less background, as well as those with greater competencies than the average student.

Additional tasks may also be included where a course or training program is specifically designed to meet the needs for a multilevel offering. In some instances, because of small student numbers, limitation of equipment, etc., the course or training program is intentionally planned to meet a number of competency level needs, or as usually referred to, a multilevel offering. This is actually a number of courses combined into one setting. This type of course or training program will be most difficult to organize effectively but must be considered, especially in the smaller educational institutions and agencies.

Even though an adequate inventory of tasks may have been obtained, the selection and development of content for use in instructional settings is not an easy undertaking. At times it is difficult to translate selected tasks into learning statements to fit specific situations. Actually, a great amount of experience by the responsible person is important in the final selection and organizing of the tasks for selected course and training programs. There is no foolproof procedure to be followed that will guarantee the accurate selecting and discarding of tasks. The process of selecting tasks requires judgment on the part of the analyzer and course developer, based upon the requirements as specified by the course or training program goals.

SEQUENCING CRITERIA AND PROCEDURES

The development of an acceptable instructional sequence of

learning tasks occurs after the appropriate tasks have been selected to be included in a specific course or training program. The accurate sequencing of tasks within a specific course is one of the more difficult procedures to carry out. It depends upon such considerations as the orientation of the course, the competency of the instructor, the background of the students, learning theory, etc. The major purpose for developing an instructional sequence is to provide the most effective and efficient learning environment for a given number of students at a given time and place.

Some courses or training programs have definite and recognizable duties or divisions which may be sequenced first, followed by a sequencing of the tasks included in each of the duties or divisions. The sequencing of the tasks, including the three classifications of *manipulative, informational,* and *attitudinal,* for each duty or division independently of the other duties or divisions is much easier than attempting to sequence the tasks for the total course at one time. Often when tasks in each duty or division are sequenced separately the results obtained may cause the title as well as the content of each duty or division to change. This happens because some tasks need to be taught early in the course even though its content may have a close relationship to tasks found in later duties or divisions. Therefore, in courses or training programs that have established duties or divisions, it is advisable to sequence these first, followed by sequencing the tasks within each.

There are many instructional areas which contain courses or training programs for which duties or divisions have not been established. In these situations, it is appropriate to sequence the total list of tasks which, in turn, will determine the establishment of the duties or divisions by grouping tasks having content that is related, those that have a similar frequency of use pattern, and also those that seem to be designed for individuals who are beginners or more advanced.

Sequencing Criteria

A number of criteria need to be considered in the sequencing process. Some of these are essentially the same criteria as used when determining the selection of tasks for inclusion in specific courses. However, they are interpreted or used to determine the placement of the task within the total course.

Each selected task (manipulative, informational, attitudinal) should be viewed as to how it meets a set of criteria designed to provide an effective learning sequence. The relationship between the various task classifications must also be considered in sequencing. In most cases each manipulative task has closely related informational tasks which need to be learned at approximately the same time. When this occurs, these tasks will need to be sequenced together even though one may not meet other sequencing criteria. This will help avoid separating informational tasks from manipulative tasks to the extent that the student cannot see the relationship and, therefore, be unable to make appropriate applications.

Selected criteria that should be used to assist in sequencing all tasks and, in turn, the respective duties or divisions include the following:

1. *Early use.* Tasks which form the basis for later tasks are presented during the early part of the course or training program. This will be true regardless whether they are difficult, complex or comprehensive.
2. *Frequency of use.* Tasks performed frequently are usually included early in the instructional offering. These, like early use, are sequenced early even though the tasks may be complex.
3. *Complexity.* The background and experience of the students will determine the placement of complex tasks to some extent. In most situations the complex tasks for a particular course are presented later in the offering and are often accomplished by those who are more advanced and highly interested in the content.
4. *Nature of student.* This criterion is very close to complexity. However, an additional consideration should be given to the type of student who will be taking the course. The goal of the student (vocational or general) will help determine the exact sequence of tasks, especially if a portion of the student's training includes an on-the-job training segment.
5. *Timing.* Often certain tasks should be sequenced in a certain order because of their relationship to other related courses where the content of both

courses can support each other and provide more effective learning for the students. Tasks may also be sequenced in a certain way to capitalize on certain types of equipment, facilities, and instructor competence which happen to be available only at certain times.

Sequencing Procedure.

The sequencing of tasks can be done mentally, recalling the criteria while visually reviewing the total list and then placing each task in a rank order sequence. However, this becomes a momentous job to accomplish, especially if the task list is lengthy.

A number of approaches, including various formats, may be used to sequence tasks quite effectively. The use of these formats will save time as well as provide a more justifiable list of sequenced learning tasks and respective duties or divisions. The approaches and formats, two of which are also used in the initial selection of essential tasks, include the following: (1) Card Approach, (2) Analysis Charting Approach, and (3) Outline Approach. Each has its merits and should be selected on the basis of how well it fits the content being considered.

Card Approach. The card approach of sequencing tasks consists of writing the title of each task, whether manipulative, informational, or attitudinal, on individual cards. Usually the tasks included in each duty or division are kept separate from those in other duties or divisions. However, if the duties or divisions have not been definitely identified, all tasks are included as one group.

If the course has an emphasis on the manipulative content, the cards containing manipulative tasks are arranged first, following the five sequence criteria, along with the acceptable order of performance when producing, maintaining, or repairing products. Each of the informational task cards are then sequenced along with the respective manipulative tasks to which they have the closest relationship. Someone very knowledgeable in the field must do the sequencing since in some cases a certain informational task must be taught first, followed by a closely related manipulative task, while in other instances the reverse may be true. The reverse of this occurs if the course content is primarily informational.

Following the arranging of both the informational and manipulative task cards, the attitudinal task cards are placed where they appear to fit in most appropriately. The attitudinal task is of such a nature that it may appear a number of times within certain duties or divisions, as well as in a number of different duties or divisions.

The advantage of the card system is that the cards can readily be rearranged as the need and the interest and level of competence required change. Following the final arrangement of the cards, the titles are typed for use in the instructional schedule or course outline.

Analysis Charting Approach. The analysis charting approach which may be used to select the essential tasks to be included in a particular course or training program may also be used to sequence the selected tasks. As when selecting tasks, the typical projects produced or activities performed are placed at the top of the chart and the selected tasks in the left hand column. The projects and activities are then analyzed and the resulting tasks included checked off. Those tasks having the greatest number of checks are usually taught first.

This approach is used primarily for content area that has a manipulative emphasis. Some adjustment will need to be made to be sure that the informational tasks fit into a logical sequence along with the respective manipulative tasks to which it has the closest relationship. Figure 5-3 which is similar to Figures 4-2 and 5-1 is an example of the analysis charting approach used to help develop a learning sequence of tasks.

Outline Approach. The outline approach is probably the most versatile of the three approaches for use in sequencing as is also true for the initial selection of the tasks for a particular course or training program. This approach may be used regardless of the instructional area, the purpose, or the level of offering.

The same format is used as when selecting the tasks. However, the rating items are changed to meet the sequencing criteria. As each task is rated against a criterion item, a numerical rating is indicated. Following this the tasks with the

ANALYSIS CHART FORMAT

Task Sequencing Form   PROJECTS/PRODUCTS

COURSE/TRAINING PROGRAM _____

TASK DESCRIPTION

		1	2	3	4	5	6	7	8	9
1										
2										
3										
4										
5										
6										
7										
8										
9										
10										
11										
12										
13										
14										
15										
16										
17										
18										
19										
20										

FIGURE 5-3

higher ratings are taught first and those with lower ratings are usually taught at a later time.

As is the case with all sequencing procedures, some adjustment will need to be made to be sure that related manipulative, informational, and attitudinal tasks are taught so that learning is most effective. Figure 5-4, which is similar to Figures 4-1 and 5-2 is an example of the outline format used for sequencing purposes.

As can be seen, in many instances the selection and se-sequencing of tasks might be done at the same time. This is especially true for courses or training programs that are not too complex or comprehensive. It is a matter of using the appropriate approach and selection/sequencing criteria so that relevant content will be obtained and sequenced.

As is the case in selecting tasks for a particular course, there is no foolproof way to carry out the sequencing process. In applying the sequencing criteria, however, one must be aware of additional factors. These might include such as the following:

1. Instructor's ability to instruct
2. Student interest and motivation
3. Student experience and background
4. Availability of facilities and equipment
5. Relationship to tasks to be learned on the job
6. Availability of time
7. Size of class
8. The changing technology
9. Extent of competency demanded

TASK DETAILING

The detailing of tasks comes only after the respective tasks for a course or training program have been appropriately selected and sequenced. The detailing of tasks involves the identification of a series of sequenced steps (elements) performed or followed in the completion of manipulative, informational, and attitudinal tasks. The steps (elements) are the smallest units into which the task content can be divided without becoming mere motions, movements, or simple mental processes.

For effective learning to occur, each task must be detailed before the instructional process begins. Through the detailing of a task, the instructor will know exactly what is to be presented, as well as what specific supporting aids and materials will be needed.

TASK SEQUENCING

Outline Format

Course/Training Programs _____ No. _____
Major Duty/Division _____ No. _____
Analyst _____ Date _____

NO.	TASK DESCRIPTION	Rating 5 (High) 4, 3, 2, 1 (Low)		
		Early	Freq.	Comp.

FIGURE 5-4

Detailing Procedure

For effective task detailing, a procedure should be established and followed to help assure that the appropriate steps and items are included. The following procedure will produce effectively detailed tasks:

1. *Verify the task.* The task to be detailed must meet the task identification criteria and be appropriate for the selected students. Each task must have at least two steps or elements.

2. *Select appropriate format.* A number of formats are available for use in detailing tasks. (These will be presented later.) The selection of the format depends upon a number of factors including the emphasis of the course and the nature of the students.

3. *Write tentative steps/elements.* A tentative task detailing for each task selected and sequenced should be done before completing the remainder of the course of study or training plan. A task detailing format should be used to accomplish this.

4. *Identify and write appropriate key points.* For each step or element of a task, there may be certain key points to be remembered. Key points are those which involve safety precautions or hazards, reminders to follow correct and accepted procedures, or the do's and don't's of the specific task and step in question.

5. *Perform or observe task being performed.* The tentative listing of the steps/elements and key points should be checked against actual performance of the task. This may change somewhat based on equipment, supplies and/or facilities available. However, an attempt should be made so that the task has universal application where possible.

6. *Have detailed task reviewed by experts.* When possible, each detailed task should be reviewed by individuals considered highly competent in that particular area. Care should be taken to make sure that the objective of the course and the needs of the students be a foremost consideration.

7. *Revise detailed task.* Based on the actual performance of the task, the review by experts, consideration of the objectives of the course and needs
of the students, the detailing of the task should be
revised. It is then ready to be used as a basis for
writing instruction sheets, development of aids,
and development of lesson or session plans.

Detailing Formats

A number of formats may be used to more effectively detail
the selected and sequenced tasks. These formats or their
adaption should be selected to fit the specific course or training program and the students to be served. Two such formats
are the (1) Two Column Format, and (2) Outline Format.

Two Column Format. The two column format which may
be used for any instructional area, level, or course emphasis, is
probably most effective for those courses where the content is
mostly manipulative. As shown in the partially completed
Figure 5-5, the procedural steps are listed in one column and
the key points are listed in the column to the right and should
be directly opposite the steps to which they relate.

It is important to include the general information as to
course/training program title, etc., so that the detailed tasks
can be organized and included in the appropriate course and
division.

Outline Format. The outline format, as is the case in its use
for selection and sequencing of tasks, is probably the most
universally appropriate. It can be effectively used for any
course or training program and within any instructional area,
whether it be vocational or general in orientation.

Figure 5-6 illustrates a partially completed outline format
used for detailing tasks. As shown, the detailing of a task requires that each major step or content element be listed. Key
points or items to remember so that effective instruction can
occur are listed under each step or element. This format has
the advantage of having all of the steps or elements and key
points listed in a sequence in which they are presented.

As is the case with the two column approach, all the general
information at the top of the page needs to be completed.
This aids in the effective filing, organizing and using the
course of study or training plan.

TASK DETAILING
Two Column Format

Course/Training Program _____General Metals_____
Major Duty/Division _____Bench Metals_____ No. _____
Task _____Layout stock_____ No. __4__ Class. __Manipulative__
Analyst _____John Watts_____ Date _____11-75_____

NO.	PROCEDURAL STEPS	KEY POINTS
1.	Select appropriate end of material	1a. Be sure end is square
		b. Remove burrs
2.	Place rule perpendicular to squared end from which measuring	2a. Rule and material end must be even
3.	Mark line on stock at correct length	3a. Use scribe
		b. Hold firmly against rule
		c. Pull scribe when marking
4.		4a.
5.		5a.

FIGURE 5-5

TASK DETAILING
Outline Format

Course/Training Program _____General Shop_____

Major Duty/Division _____Finishing_____ No. ___6___

Task ___Identify kinds of abrasives___ No. ___3___ Class. __Informational__

Analyst _____John Watts_____ Date ___11-75___

NO.	STEPS/TOPICS AND KEY POINTS
1.	Kinds of abrasives
	a. Garnet
	b. Flint
	c. Steel wood
	d. Emery cloth
2.	Characteristics of garnet
	a. Contains grains of garnet
	b. Very hard material
	c. Expensive
	d.
	e.
3.	Characteristics of flint
	a.
	b.
	c.
	d.
	e.

FIGURE 5-6

SUMMARY

The accurate selection of learning tasks, their sequencing according to appropriate criteria, and the detailing of these tasks are the basis for courses and training programs.

The tabulation of data received, whether done by machine or by hand, must be performed accurately since it is the base for data interpretation. Selected criteria, including an appropriate cut-off value, is used in relationship to a specific offering when interpreting data received through the inventory of tasks. Following this tabulation the selection of tasks for specific courses or training programs is carried out.

The selection of tasks for a course or training program is based upon a number of criteria including (1) frequency of performance and use, (2) importance and need, (3) basic and required, (4) complexity and difficulty, (5) immediacy, (6) time element, (7) appropriateness for setting, (8) duplication, and (9) meet task statement criteria. Limitations such as availability of funds, space, and equipment must also be considered when selecting suitable tasks. The analysis chart and outline are two formats that may be used to aid in the actual selection of tasks from the total inventory of tasks.

The sequencing of tasks occurs after they have been selected to fit a particular offering. The total listing of tasks for a course may be sequenced or those tasks in each duty or division may be sequenced separately. Regardless of the approach, the following criteria should be considered along with the use of either the card approach, analysis charting approach, or the outline approach: (1) early use, (2) frequency of use, (3) complexity, (4) nature of student, and (5) timing.

Following the selecting and sequencing of the tasks, each is detailed to be used as a basis for instruction sheet, instructional aid, and lesson or session plan development. A specific procedure should be followed to assure accurate task detailing. The detailing of tasks is more easily accomplished if either the two column or outline format is used.

SUGGESTED QUESTIONS AND ACTIVITIES

1. State several reasons why a tabulation form should be developed at the same time that the inventory of tasks is developed.

2. Establish a cut-off average or percentage you plan to use as a criterion for retaining tasks. Justify the cut-off point for your particular instructional area and students to be served.

3. Aside from the selection criteria, there are a number of limitations that must be considered when selecting tasks for a course. List and rank these in order as they will affect your course.

4. Nine criteria to be considered when selecting tasks for a

course were presented. Which six do you think are most appropriate for your course? Justify your answer.

5. Develop a procedure you plan to follow in selecting tasks for a particular course or training program. Adapt one of the formats presented to meet your specific needs.

6. List the advantage and disadvantages of both the Analysis Chart Format and the Outline Format for use in selecting tasks.

7. Present a number of reasons why it is important to sequence selected tasks in an instructional order.

8. Rank the presented sequencing criteria in order of use in sequencing tasks. Explain your reason for this ranking.

9. If you have each of the three classification of tasks in a particular course or training program, which one will take precedence in the sequencing procedure? How will the other two be treated? Why?

10. Explain how, why, and when you would use each of the three sequencing approaches (Card, Analysis Charting, Outline).

11. Develop a format designed to help you sequence the task for your course. Use the format for at least one duty or division.

12. State at least three reasons why each task in a course should be detailed before actual instruction begins.

13. Develop a task detailing format you will use for detailing tasks in your course or training program. Select two tasks each of manipulative and information, and, using your format, detail each task.

CHAPTER 6

Performance Objectives

F or many years, educators and trainers have stated goals, aims, or purposes for courses, curriculums and programs. Traditionally, many of these have been very vague or general, giving some overall directions to learning but lacking the specificity necessary for effective instruction and its evaluation.

Instructors have typically developed goals or objectives for a particular course or lesson directed at what they planned to do rather than what the students were to accomplish. Often many of these goals, as well as objectives for selected instructional content, were developed without reference to the subject matter and the institution's or agency's goals and philosophy. These did provide some direction for learning but frequently were not clear nor very well understood, especially by the students.

The initiation and the use of performance objectives by instructors has aided materially in the effective conduct and learning of content. The use of performance objectives has provided both the instructor and the student a base for common understanding which, in turn, has not only caused more relevant instruction and evaluation, but also greater involvement by the student in the learning process.

This chapter contains content designed to provide an opportunity to gain an understanding of the place, importance and use of performance objectives in the learning process. The specific topics are: (1) Goals and Objectives, (2) Performance Objective Components and Criteria, and (3) Writing the Performance Objective.

CHAPTER OBJECTIVES

Through the study of this chapter and the completion of suggested questions and activities, you will have accomplished the following objectives. You will be able to:

1. Accurately differentiate between goals, learning tasks, and performance objectives, and explain the functions, advantages, and disadvantages of each.
2. List and describe the specific characteristics and functions of each of the component parts of a performance objective.
3. Identify acceptable from non-acceptable performance objective statements and rewrite non-acceptable objectives so that they meet performance objectives criteria.
4. Provided with listed tasks, write acceptable performance objectives for each of the classifications of (1) information, (2) manipulative, (3) attitudinal.

GOALS AND OBJECTIVES

Performance objectives for content included in lessons, units, or courses are an outgrowth of the stated goals or purposes of a subject or curriculum area. It is essential to first identify or understand the goals of the instruction, as well as the philosophy of the agency or institution before acceptable and relevant performance objectives can be written.

Goals

Goals, which are sometimes referred to as broad objectives, form the framework for performance objectives. They are broad general outcomes of instruction which do not state or convey meaning in a behavioral sense. As emphasized in an earlier chapter, before an appropriate analysis can be conducted, the broad objectives or goals of the instructional area, or a part of this area under consideration, must be identified. Only after this has been accomplished can the specific tasks be selected for which performance objectives are written. Curriculum and program planning require goal statements. These statements, however, give little assistance to the instructor for a specific class or laboratory setting. These goal statements include or encompass the specific performance objectives which can be used by the instructor in specific instructional settings.

Therefore, goal statements which are general outcomes of instruction do provide the overall guidelines for instruction but not the specifics needed to effectively evaluate that instruction. Goals do not specifically tell what the students will do at the end of instruction. Goals primarily serve in setting the parameters of the instruction and the starting point for developing performance objectives. Goal statements also serve as a means of communication between professionals and non-professionals, as well as summarizing the purposes of programs and curriculums. It is important to know the instructional goals of a program or course. However, these are not adequate for use in effectively developing and evaluating selected instructional content.

Examples of Goals: The following are examples of goal statements representing various levels of instructional content. As will be noted, none is specific enough for use as the prime base for instruction or evaluation:

1. To become a productive citizen.
2. Develop a degree of skill in the use of tools.
3. Develop an understanding of employee-employer relations.
4. Understanding safety procedure in the class and laboratory.
5. Develop attitudes of cooperation and consideration with fellow students.
6. Develop competence in the operation of test equipment.
7. Develop skill in the use of automotive tune-up equipment.
8. Gain an understanding of materials and processes of industry.

Objectives

Objectives, when stated in a very broad sense, serve the same function as do goals, aims, or purposes. However, when objectives become more specific and narrow in scope they serve the function of describing, rather precisely, what the content will be, what responsibilities students and instructors have, and the nature of the evaluation process.

Performance objectives are written after the goals have been stated and the content has been selected through the identification of the learning tasks. The learning tasks are the base for the performance objectives. Task statements are not the same as performance objectives. Listed tasks for a particular content segment indicate what is included in the course or training program, while the performance objectives state the expected performance level or standard to be met at at the end of the instructional period.

Performance objectives represent the intentions, the expectations, and the aspirations of both the instructor and the students as related to the content under study. They are stated in terms of how the student will perform rather than what the instructor intends to do. Performance objectives provide a guide and, indirectly, motiviation for the improvement of instruction. Well formed performance objectives help to reduce the confusion often associated with instructional planning. The less ambiguity surrounding a statement of educational outcomes, the easier it is to develop effective instruction. A clear statement of objectives helps the instructor to select appropriate activities to be used in instructional courses and programs. They aid the student and instructor to better organize activities and efforts leading to the kinds of performances desired. Performance objectives are concerned with the performance of the students rather than with reference books read, activities completed, or the performance of the instructor.

Some major identifiable functions of performance objectives in relationship to course and training program development are: (1) describes the desired behavior of the student at the completion of the instructional period, (2) serves to coordinate and integrate the diverse activities of all those involved in the instructional process, (3) provides a document that shows a systematic development of instruction, (4) provides a standard against which the student can be evaluated, and (5) emphasizes the end product rather than the means of arriving there; that is, output by the student rather than input by the instructor.

Performance objectives provide an indication of the destination to be reached by students in their educational and training program. They are the specific statements of purpose which provide direction for the instructor or an indication of accomplishment for the student.

There are numerous benefits that are derived from the use of performance objectives, as well as a number of disadvantages. Some of the identifiable advantages of performance objectives include the following:

1. Both students and instructors have a clear understanding as to the direction that the content will take.
2. Students are more accepting of instructor's judgment when evaluated against performance objectives.
3. A greater amount of independent study is permitted and unstructured learning procedures are available.
4. Performance objectives cause greater communication between all populations.
5. More effective and closely related teaching methods and techniques can be identified and used.
6. They form the base for the development of criterion tests.
7. They provide a system for continuous evaluation throughout the course or training program.
8. Tend to be motivators for more effective learning.

Some of the disadvantages of performance objectives include the following:

1. Too much concentration on the lower levels of objectives, especially those that require mere memorization.
2. A tendency to overemphasize the manipulative and informational content and underemphasize the attitudinal content.

3. Difficulty in objectively evaluating some of the performance objectives that attempt to measure the higher levels of learning.
4. Writing performance objectives is very time consuming, especially during the early stages.
5. The inability of most instructors to write performance objectives that can be readily understood by all those involved in the learning process.

PERFORMANCE OBJECTIVE COMPONENTS AND CRITERIA

Correctly written performance objectives contain four major components which designate: (1) the student, (2) behavior, (3) condition, and (4) level of performance. The four components must be either specifically stated or implied if the objective is to meet the criteria of a performance objective and function effectively for both the student and the instructor.

Like task statements, performance objectives can be classified as manipulative, informational, and attitudinal. Performance objectives are written for all tasks in a course or training program which, therefore, causes them to be classified in the same manner. An acceptable and an appropriate performance objective only occurs if a well written task statement is used as its base. Therefore, well written and appropriately selected tasks must be available before the performance objective writing begins.

Performance Objective Components

The performance objective contains four parts or components which, when combined in a suitable sequence, provide a statement that indicates to students and others the learning that is to take place. The four components are (1) the student, (2) the behavior which the student exhibits, (3) the condition under which the student performs, and (4) the performance level which the student must achieve.

The Student. Each objective must specify the individual or individuals to whom the objective is directed. Performance objectives are directed to the student receiving the instruction rather than to the instructor who is presenting the instruction.

An objective statement such as "identify kinds of materials used" does not include an indication who the student is and, therefore, would not be acceptable. In some cases, the student(s) may be implied because of a previous statement or an explanation within the course of study or training plan. It must be clear, however, to whom the objectives are directed. Often courses have students of various backgrounds and competency levels enrolled in them. If this is the case specific statements indicating the students to be involved for a specific objective must be made. Statements such as the following should be used:

1. All 11th grade students in Graphic Arts II will . . .
2. Freshmen community college students enrolled in Electronics 101 will . . .
3. Students completing Unit I in the Construction Course will . . .

Behavior. The behavior component of the performance objective refers to the overt behavior of a student. To verify that learning has taken place one must be able to either observe the actual behavior or the results from the student's actions. The behavior observed or the results of actions must be so stated that instructors of like subject matter areas would be able to interpret the behavior and evaluate it somewhat uniformly.

For a statement to be written that can be interpreted in the same manner by students and instructors alike, certain words and phrases used to indicate overt actions must be used.

General words such as *know, understand, like, appreciate, learn, grasp, comprehend, want, taste, feel,* etc., are words that that sound important but have different meanings for various individuals. For the objective to be readily understood by those immediately involved (students and instructors), words that describe behavior must be action oriented words, providing for evaluation by observing the specific behavior or the product of the behavior.

Some of the action oriented words that may be used effectively in describing the behavior component of performance objectives include the following:

compute	drill	specify
define	type	state
estimate	mix	volunteer
list	greet	modify
construct	smile	transfer
measure	select	value
identify	describe	create

The behavior component of the performance objective tells what is to be accomplished as an end product and not the process used to attain that end product. However, broad performance objectives may be written which actually contain a series of sub-objectives or more narrow objectives. As each of these narrow objectives is completed, it may be thought of as a step in the process of completed and more broadly stated performance objectives.

Statements which illustrate the correct usage of words for the behavior component include the following:

1. Each student will be able to *list* the names of . . . .
2. All students will *construct,* according to plans, . . .
3. When provided with the tools, students will *measure* each sample to an accuracy of . . . .

By specifying an observable behavior in an objective the instructor greatly reduces ambiguity regarding the intent of the instruction.

Condition. It is important for the student to know under what circumstances that the objective is to be completed. The component, *condition,* refers to the environmental aspects of the performance situation under which the objective is to be performed. Conditions may be thought of as limiting factors or as restraints placed upon the students. The component *condition* specifies exactly what is to be used or employed by the student in performing the objective and within what environment it is to be done.

In some instances the condition may be understood, which often occurs in the more academic oriented classroom. However, in most cases, condition(s) must be stated so that the student knows exactly the when, where, and how of the expected performance, and so that the instructor can evaluate fairly and uniformily. If the course or training program has a vocational emphasis, the specified conditions must approximate the actual on-the-job situation. The major emphasis should be on realism as much as possible. The more the performance required in the objective deviates from the actual work conditions, the more the validity of the training should be questioned.

Following are several partial statements that illustrate the manner in which the condition component of the performance objective is stated:

1. *Using a key punch and the manufacturing manual,* each student will . . . .
2. *Given the necessary tools,* the employee will . . . .
3. *Following the completion of Unit 5,* each student will . . . .

Performance Level. The standard of performance, usually referred to when writing performance objectives as "level of performance," in completing the performance objective must also be stated in terms that can be understood by both the instructor and the student. The *level of performance* as used in performance objectives refers to an acceptable minimal standard of achievement as viewed by the individual(s) who developed and those who agreed to the objective.

The establishment of the level of performance is most often done by the instructor based upon input from various sources. In some instances the selected standard or level may be modified by the students or as a result of reviewing the background abilities and intentions of students enrolled in the particular course for which the performance objectives have been written.

A major purpose of a performance objective is to communicate what will be and, later, what has been accomplished after the completion of a segment of content. In occupational courses and training programs it is essential that the employing agency knows the standard or level of accomplishment attained by those involved in the program. This implies that the consumer (the employer) of the product (the student completing the unit, course, training program, etc.) has some input in establishing the level of performance. Therefore, course developers must consult with the students who are or will be enrolled, and also the employers, in the establishment of the standards to be written into performance objectives.

Some examples of performance level statements follow:

1. .... solder two pieces ..... *with no air bubbles and a resulting shiny smooth seam.*
2. .... *and making no more than 10 errors.*
3. .... *complete activity in thirty minutes.*

Performance levels specify the degree of success needed to meet the objective. Performance levels answer questions such as: (1) what degree of accuracy must be attained? (2) what percentage of the items must be identified? (3) what time limitation must be met? Regardless of what the stated required performance level includes, it must be understood and accepted by all of the persons included in the offering. Ideally, the performance level will change as the backgrounds of individuals differ and the demand for various competencies change.

Performance Objective Criteria

Criteria should be established, reviewed, and matched against objective statements to insure that they are truly performance objective statements. If performance objectives are to be used as a basis for student and instructor evaluation they must be as objective as possible and relevant to the content and process under study.

The first major set of criteria to be met is the inclusion of the four components described in the previous section. Each component must be so stated that all involved understand exactly what is expected.

The second set of criteria used to evaluate acceptable performance objectives to be considered included the following:

1. *Levels of Writing.* The stated objective is to fit the group to whom it is addressed. Language in the objective must be understood by the students and others involved.

2. *Product vs. Process.* The performance objective deals with the end product, the result of the activity completed by students. This permits various approaches to be used by students in accomplishing a certain standard. The instructor has the responsibility for providing the accepted process so that the end product, whether manipulative, informational, or attitudinal, is achieved.

3. *Observable.* Regardless of what is attempted, as spelled out by the objectives, the result must be observable in some way before it can be accepted and used as a basis for evaluation. The actions observed must be such that they can be interpreted in a quantified manner and in a way that objective evaluation can be made.

4. *Action Oriented.* All performance objectives are action oriented. This requires that students perform in such a way that results can be observed. A well stated task, using a command form style, provides the action portion of the performance objective.

5. *Specific.* Unlike goal statements which are broad and somewhat all inclusive, performance objectives are specific and somewhat narrow and limited in scope. Performance objectives are written for each task or a combination of tasks which are very similar. Performance objectives may be written for courses which are in reality very broad. For instructional purposes, however, the performance objective is rather specific.

6. *Realistic.* The objectives must be realisitic in terms of the student's abilities, aspirations, and interests. Also, they should be realistic in terms of time involved, as well as materials, etc., to be used. This criterion will cause certain performance objectives to be changed as the students and the technology itself change. The objective must also be realistic in terms of the employer and his needs.

7. *Worthy.* This criterion is closely related to that of being realistic. The student must feel that the objective is worthy of accomplishing and one that

meets his short and/or long range goals. At certain academic levels, students may not realize the value or worth of certain selected objectives. In these cases, the instructor has the responsibility of providing this background to the student and showing the importance and relationships.

8. *Financially feasible.* Course and training programs should be developed to meet ideal situations, including the performance objective statement. However, when introducing a certain segment of content in a selected setting, the financial aspects need to be considered. In some cases, the content, and in turn the performance objectives, will need to be revised to meet the practical situation that exists. Often certain tasks, because of costs, are relegated to the actual work situation rather than be included in a more formal training program. When this occurs the objective, as a course requirement, will need to be removed unless a cooperative arrangement has been established, including the evaluation of the performance on the job.

9. *Consistent with the job.* All performance objectives are written to be consistent or within the framework of the institution, department, instructional area, subject, and course goals. One of the major purposes of the performance objectives is to help assure that the stated goals will be attained. The performance objectives might be thought of as the steps to be followed in completion of the goal statements.

To be effective, performance objectives should meet the above-listed criteria. In some cases a certain objective may not meet all of the listed criteria, which will tend to cause some problems and misunderstanding among those individuals involved.

WRITING THE PERFORMANCE OBJECTIVE

The actual writing of the performance objectives to fit

specific situations is relatively easy if the difference between them and goals is known, and if the component parts and criteria of performance objectives are thoroughly understood. The writing of performance objectives involves the breaking down of broad program, course or unit goals into smaller components that are stated in specific terms. These which use the task statements as a base become the performance objectives. It must be remembered that each of the specific performance objectives must contribute to the goal(s) statement for the content under study.

Responsibilities for Writing

The major responsibility for writing the performance objectives designed for specific content areas is that of the instructor. When instructors write objectives it helps them to define more clearly exactly what will be included and emphasized during the course of instruction. Just because instructors have this responsibility does not mean that they can do this in isolation from their students or without consideration of the stated goals and philosophy of the subject area or institution.

It has been found that instructors who develop and write their own objectives tend to perform more effectively in an instructional setting. It brings to light possible new approaches in presenting and coordinating instruction. Also, the accountability phase of the instructional process is brought more clearly into focus and becomes more definitive for both the instructor and the student.

The learning responsibility rests with the student while making provisions for effective learning rests with the instructor. This implies that once content has been identified as being essential, some means needs to be developed for the evaluation of whether the prescribed content was actually learned. One of the major steps in the process of assuring that learning did take place is the writing of objectives in performance form.

Since, by and large, students do not have the knowledge, background, or time to develop their own set of objectives to the detail necessary, the writing of objectives does become the responsibility of the instructor. However, depending upon particular situations, students should have some input regarding the adaptation of prescribed objectives to fit their particular needs and interests.

The writing of performance objectives by instructors is a major means of communicating directly to the students regarding exactly what the particular course or training program is all about. The instructor is saying, "This is the content to be studied for which you (students) will be held accountable." If the instructor has followed acceptable procedures in selecting content, the objectives will tend to be relevant and acceptable to the students. The levels of performing, however, may need to be adjusted to fit particular needs. The clear statement of objectives relieves the students from spending their energies in attempting to "second guess" what their instructor expects of them. Therefore, the writing of the performance objectives is clearly that of the instructor, whereas the learning of the content so that the objectives can be attained is that of the students.

Writing Suggestions

A major requirement for writing performance objectives is that it be in the language which can easily be understood by those who become involved in its use. Even though content may be quite similar for two different groups of students, the language and sentence structure may need to be changed due to the difference in the background and abilities of the students. This does not mean that the performance level expected would be lowered. Rather, the objectives would be stated in such a way that effective communication with each of the students will result. The reading level of the students must be ascertained and the objective written to fit that level.

Each of the four components of performance objectives must be specifically stated or clearly indicated for each objective written. Also, each of the criteria discussed in the previous section must be considered so that an objective is written that fits the content and the individual student.

One of the disadvantages of writing performance objectives is the problem of redundancy of certain statements or words, especially if the objectives are quite narrow in scope. The objective writer should consider using a single statement that might indicate the student, the condition, etc., if these are the same for all or a portion of a certain set of objective statements. This single statement is then followed by a number of statements which include only those components that change for each performance objective statement. For example, if all of the instruction takes place in a formal classroom and applies to the same students, a prestatement to be used with all the objectives might be, "All students in Electronics Course 3B, following the completion of Unit 4, will . . . . ." Specific statements could be made indicating only the expected behavior as related to the content and the level of performance to be met by the students.

Performance objectives are also written to reflect different levels of learning which relate directly to the tasks identified and included in the course or training program. The lower level performance objectives deal with such things as listing, recalling, identifying, selecting, attaching, removing, etc. Unfortunately, most performance objectives in the past have been written at this level.

If competency in problem solving, analysis, judgment, etc., is to be the outcome of an instructional offering, then the performance objectives must reflect this. This means that the instructor must identify exactly what the desired competencies are to be and write performance objectives that will effectively communicate this to the students and will, in turn, indicate the evaluation level and procedure. Such objectives will contain action words such as *solve, fabricate, design, explain, predict, judge, build,* etc.

When writing objectives, the instructor should remember that each performance objective is based upon an identified task or several closely related tasks. Each objective must meet the listed criteria and be so written that the message communicated is understood by all individuals involved. Performance objectives are the base for all evaluation, indicating that they must be precisely written to include the level of performance required.

Regardless of the breadth or length of a performance objective statement, to be effective it contains the essential component parts and meets the listed criteria. It has been emphasized that the instructor is responsible for the writing of performance objectives for a particular course. However, more effective objectives will result if more than one person is involved in their development. Team writing of objectives has great merit. This helps to assure that expertise in the specialized content (in breadth) as well as in learning theory and writing ability is available.

Performance objectives may be written for courses, training programs, units, lessons, etc. The more narrow the content is in scope, the more specific the performance objective becomes. Performance objectives for courses tend to involve more problem solving, application, evaluation, etc., than is the case for performance objectives written for a specific task. In practice, however, most instructors write descriptive goal statements for particular courses or training programs, followed by performance objectives for each of the units and/or lessons or sessions. In some cases the unit objectives are actually sub-goal statements, thus leaving the lesson or session with specifically stated performance objectives.

Examples of Performance Objectives

As indicated earlier, performance objectives reflect informational, manipulative, and attitudinal content. For effective evaluation, each objective must be directed to only one of the three classifications.

The following is a somewhat broadly stated performance objective developed for use in a short workshop session:

"Given appropriate guidelines, each workshop participant will write two performance objectives which meet the standards set by the workshop director."

The above objective is informational. Each of the four components are included and stated to communicate exactly what is expected. The component parts are:

Student:	workshop participants
Behavior:	write two performance objectives
Condition:	given appropriate guidelines
Level:	meet the standards set by the workshop director

The following performance objectives are also classified as

informational, and contain the four component parts, but stated in a little different manner:

Each student will, with 100% accuracy, list names of all the engine components included in auto tune-up without reference to any manuals or visual aids.

Following completion of Unit 3, each student, with the use of an oscilloscope, will be able to correctly measure and record the current gain in an NPN and PNP transistor as judged by the instructor.

Provided with appropriate reference materials, students will demonstrate knowledge of the purpose of fillets, rounds, and runouts by inclusion and dimensioning on assigned drawing of machined castings, meeting predetermined standards.

In most instances, performance objectives covering manipulative content are more easily written than those included in either of the other two classifications. This is mainly because the overt behavior is more easily observed. Following are some examples of acceptable performance objectives covering manipulative content:

Provided with needed equipment and materials, each student in course 5A will rip cut a board along a line not varying more than the width of a saw blade.

Given the necessary instruction and provided with needed equipment, each Auto 4 student will balance two wheels following procedures and meeting standards stated in the manual.

Each student in Session 3, selecting appropriate tools, and provided with materials and specifications, will drill two holes not varying more than 1/32 of an inch from the listed specifications.

Performance objectives for attitudinal content are most difficult to write because of the general inability to actually see the resulting overt behavior or product of the behavior of the students. If, however, attitudinal content is important and essential for the particular course or training program, it then must be included and appropriate objectives written. Following are some examples of attitudinal performance objectives:

After the completion of Unit 1 and 2, each student will indicate a positive attitude toward shop safety by voluntarily following posted safety rules.

Within the laboratory setting, students will show cooperativeness and willingness in working with others who are exhibiting problems by securing needed manuals and reference materials, voluntarily showing and explaining their use to others in need of this assistance.

All drafting students will demonstrate their respect for drafting equipment by properly maintaining and storing equipment issued to them as judged by the instructor according to established laboratory regulations.

SUMMARY

Instruction at all levels and in the various disciplines have traditionally attempted to convey to their students the purposes of the content of their courses. This has been in the form of goals, purposes, aims, and objectives. It has been found, to be effective, that these must be expressed in the terms of the students and in language that they can understand.

Goals are used to describe broad general outcomes of instruction and are developed within the framework of stated philosophy. They provide the parameters of the instruction and the starting point for developing performance objectives.

Performance objectives describe precisely what the content will accomplish and the responsibilities of the students and the instructor. Performance objectives are written only after the goals have been identified and learning tasks selected. Performance objectives represent the intentions, expectation, and aspirations of participants in the area of study. Some major functions of performance objectives include: (1) they describe required student behavior, (2) coordinate diverse activities, (3) systematic development of materials, (4) basis for evaluation, and (5) emphasize the product rather than the process.

Correctly written performance objectives contain the four major components of student identification, student behavior, conditions under which performed, and the level of performance required. These objectives must be specific, easily understood, observable, action oriented, realistic, worthy, and financially feasible.

The writing of performance objectives is the responsibility of the instructor. Effective performance objectives are based upon the needs and interests of the students involved. Performance objectives are a means of communication between the instructor and the students. This requires that performance objectives must be clearly understood by all concerned. This is especially important since they are the basis for eventual evaluation of student performance.

Performance objectives like the tasks can be classified as informational, manipulative, and attitudinal. Performance objectives are written for various levels of learning including the lower level, where recall and routine skills are emphasized, to higher levels emphasizing problem solving, creating, and fabricating. Primarily, performance objectives are developed to communicate what will be covered in a selected offering and how the competency gained will be evaluated.

SUGGESTED QUESTIONS AND ACTIVITIES

1. Explain the place of goals and their use in the instructional program (program of studies, curriculum, course of study/training plan).

2. List the major functions that goals serve within particular institutions or training agencies.

3. Write a set of goal statements for your subject field, for your course.

4. Make a list, in priority order, of the major functions served by performance objectives.

5. List five specific advantages that performance objectives contribute to the beginning teacher.

6. State the four components included in an acceptable performance objective. Write a statement that will illustrate each component.

7. Make a list of key action words for each classification that may be used to describe the behavior component. Rate each as to its level of learning required.

8. Explain each of the criteria listed as to its importance for consideration when writing performance objectives.

9. Write two performance objectives to represent each of the three classifications (information, manipulative, attitudinal). Classify each as to the level of learning it represents. Explain.

10. Obtain a list of objectives presently used in a selected course. Identify those that are acceptable performance objectives. Rewrite those that are not written in acceptable form.

11. Identify a particular unit in a course (preferably one you are developing). For this unit write acceptable performance objectives that meet all criteria.

Part III
Development
And Application

chapter 7

Instructional Schedules

The identification and sequencing of course or training content for a specific offering to meet the needs of selected students is one of the major requirements for effective instruction. However, this identification and sequencing of content (learning tasks) does not go far enough in providing an organized approach necessary for the eventual implementation of a specific offering.

The content selected must be organized in such a manner that it can be easily presented and with little confusion. Such an organized approach may result in an appropriate outline including the listing of all aids, references, assignments, projects, instruction sheets, etc., to be used in conjunction with specified learning tasks. This type of organization of materials provides the instructor with an instructional schedule which, if followed, with some flexibility, will provide for more effective instruction and a greater learning opportunity for students.

This chapter deals with the development and organization of course or training content and materials into a usable instructional schedule. The specific topics covered include the following: (1) Importance and Use, (2) Instructional Schedule Components, and (3) Instructional Schedule Formats.

CHAPTER OBJECTIVES

Through the study of this chapter and the completion of suggested questions and activities, you will accomplish the following objectives. You will be able to:

133

1. List and explain at least ten major purposes and reasons for using instructional schedules.
2. Identify and justify appropriate components to be included in an instructional schedule designed to meet specific educational offerings (i.e., vocational, general, laboratory, etc.).
3. Describe the purpose and indicate the appropriate placement of each component included in an instructional schedule.
4. Plan, develop, and complete an instructional schedule to meet the specific requirements of a selected course or training program.

IMPORTANCE AND USE

A major obstacle facing most instructors who are very proficient in their field is the difficulty of presenting their knowledge and skills in an orderly and effective manner to their students. The instructor must not only be sure that the content being presented is needed and essential, but also that the content is organized in such a way that it has continuity between the various kinds of tasks (manipulative, informational, and attitudinal), and that all the aids, methods, devices, etc., used relate as directly as possible to specific tasks being presented.

The instructional schedule provides a vehicle through which an organized and systematic approach can be developed and followed in presenting content effectively. The instructional schedule may be very comprehensive, including a listing of everything that will be used and taught in a course or training program, or it may be quite brief, including only a listing of a few support devices besides the learning tasks.

Some of the reasons for the development and use of an instructional schedule include the following:

1. Provides a format for the sequenced listing of the learning tasks for the specific offering.
2. Presents the tasks in a psychological and logical learning sequence.
3. Shows the relationship between the materials, aids, and devices used in an offering.

4. Shows the relationship between the support materials and devices, and the learning tasks.
5. Provides a quick overview of the offering for use by administration and for evaluation purposes.
6. It can be used as a basis for instruction when time is limited for developing the comprehensive course of study or training plan.
7. It serves as a basis and guide for further instructional materials development.
8. It provides for the inclusion of such items or indicators as time and content emphasis.
9. Provides an easily used format which permits changes to be made as technology, methodology, etc., changes.
10. Permits instructors to view needs well ahead of schedule so that materials, visual aids, etc., may be secured in sufficient time.

INSTRUCTIONAL SCHEDULE COMPONENTS

The instructional schedule may include a great number of components or a very few depending upon its intended use. There are a basic set of components that all instructional schedules should include regardless of its purpose. As courses or training programs become more complex, the instructional schedule becomes more comprehensive. The instructor needs to identify those components beyond the basic ones which are absolutely necessary to help assure that the instruction is most effective and the learning is emphasized.

The instructional schedule is designed to be an aid to the instructor in the overall planning and organizing of the comprehensive course of study or training plan. With this in mind, it is important that the schedule is designed to meet the specific needs of the students and the particular instructional situation. Therefore, the components of instructional schedules may change beyond the basic ones as the content, emphasis, students, etc., change.

The components of the instructional schedule are divided into two groups, (1) the minimum components required, and (2) those considered optional but desirable. The following components make up the instructional schedule, with the first four being considered as required:

1. Course/training title
2. Division/duty
3. Tasks
4. Time
5. Methods
6. Audio/visual aids
7. Activities
8. Written instruction sheets
9. Text and references
10. Evaluative devices

Formats which include a combination of these components are presented in the next section of this chapter. Instructional schedules that include only the minimum number of components are often referred to as course or training outlines.

Course/Training Title

The course or training program title should appear on each sheet used in the instructional schedule. This will help avoid confusion and facilitate the assembly and use of the schedule. The title should be definitive and the same as used by the institution or agency through which it is conducted.

Division/Duty

The division or duty number and title must also appear on the instructional schedule sheets so that they can be kept in the correct order for use in the instructional situation. It is most desirable that each new division or duty begin on a separate sheet as this provides the instructor the opportunity to organize the materials by major sections (division/duty). In some cases, especially content areas which are highly informational, the term "unit" may be used to replace the term "division".

Tasks

The tasks are listed in sequential learning order, as determined by the instructor, under each division or duty to which they apply. Tasks may be numbered consecutively only within the division or duty, or for the total course or training program.

In most cases the manner in which the task was stated during the time it was identified, selected, and sequenced is the same manner that it is stated in the instructional schedule. However, depending upon the situation and the preferences of the instructor, the task statement in the instructional schedule may be stated in topic form. Topic form statements do not necessarily follow the criterion of task statements, that of being stated in a command form using an action verb.

The following are several examples of statements using specific task statement criteria and using the topic statement format.

Task Statement	Topic Statement
1. Identify kinds and use of abrasive materials	1. Kinds and use of abrasive materials
2. Rip cut to a line	2. Sawing stock
3. Disassemble and assemble carburetor	3. Maintain carburetors
4. List laboratory safety rules	4. Safety rules

As will be noted, the most desirable approach is to list the specific tasks in the accepted format. When stated in this manner, both the instructor and the student know exactly what will be presented and what is to be learned. The topic method provides statements which might well cause confusion as to exactly what the content really does include. This, in turn, will cause misunderstanding at the time of evaluation.

The instructional schedule is more accurate and more usable if a provision is made to identify the classification of each task. This might be a designation following each task statement with letters "M" for manipulative tasks, "I" for informational tasks, and "A" for attitudinal tasks. In some schedules, special columns are provided for each classification in which the proper one is checked opposite the respective tasks.

Time

It is quite essential not only to estimate the time for the total offering but also for each segment (division/duty) and, in some cases, for each learning task. This provides the instructor with guidelines that will help to place emphasis where it should be.

When developing a course or training program the instructor should know the total time available and be aware of the possible interruptions which will cause a decrease in the total time frame. During the initial developmental stages, time is considered secondary to the selection of learning content (tasks) for use in an offering. However, when the instructional schedule is being developed, a very realistic look must be taken of the exact amount of time available.

It is very easy for instructors to overemphasize their specialty and de-emphasize those areas in which they have little interest or in which they lack proficiency. A well organized and developed instructional schedule will help to avoid this. It will or should include a minimum time listing for each division or duty and where possible, a tentative time identification for each task or group of related tasks.

For some offerings which are highly shop or laboratory oriented, the time identification might be indicated separately for classroom and shop or laboratory activities. The use of this approach depends somewhat on the nature and purpose of the offering (general or vocational) as well as type of students and the facilities available.

It can be seen that it is most important to include the time element in the instructional schedule. The more accurate it can be made, the more effective the instruction will be.

Methods

The instructional schedule becomes much more usable and valuable to the instructor as additional information is added. One of the major reasons why tasks are classified as manipulative, informational, or attitudinal is that each different classification requires the use of different types of methods or techniques in its presentation. Often the instructor does not indicate the specific methods to use if it is obvious that only certain ones apply.

The designated method does provide the instructor, however, with an immediate visual input regarding how to present each task or group of related tasks. As in the case with task classification, each method might be indicated by using the first letter of each method classification (i.e., "L" for lecture, "D" for demonstration, etc.).

Audio/Visual Aids

The entry of audio/visual aids, opposite the tasks to which they relate directly, is probably one of the more important entries since so many aids of various kinds are being used. The major purpose of audio/visual aids (films, pictures, tapes, radio, models, etc.) is to supplement and support rather than replace instruction.

A major purpose for providing space to indicate the audio/visual aids is that it provides the instructor with a complete listing needed at the beginning of the course or training program. This provides lead time for the instructor in developing or ordering the necessary aids. It also provides a space for indicating and adding new aids which will be used in presenting content, as these aids become available. The listing of these aids does provide a complete picture of the various aids needed for the course or training plan during its offering.

Activities

A column in the instructional schedule is most often provided for the listing of appropriate activities that are to be carried out by students in the process of learning the course or training program content. Activities include those items which are considered "means to an end." Therefore, this column would include a listing of such things as projects, jobs, exercises, problems, experiments, assignments, etc.

A great amount of discussion has been and is being held regarding the advisability and suitability of various types of activities, especially projects and jobs. When the instructor uses these types of activities to assist and motivate students in learning the identified content more effectively, it makes little difference which ones and how many become part of the course or training program as long as they are used to promote the learning of the selected content.

A separate column should be provided for the activities to be included in the offering. They are listed opposite the task which is the first one learned or practiced in the completion of the particular activity. Only one activity for a complete division or duty may be specified for certain offerings, while in others a great number of various kinds of activities will be included.

If a course or training program has a great many written assignments these are indicated and placed in a separate column. This often occurs in offerings that are primarily informational oriented.

Written Instruction Sheets

Most course offerings, especially in the industrial and technical field, include a great number of prepared (either by the instructor or commercially) written instruction sheets. This is especially true in new and emerging subject area, and in those offerings designed to prepare students to meet the demands of a more locally oriented area.

Written instruction sheets, like the other components of an instructional schedule, are placed opposite the specific task(s) to which they apply. Because titles of the sheets may be lengthy, a code system is frequently used to indicate that an instruction sheet will be used.

In most instances, instructors do not have sufficient time to prepare all the required instruction sheets. However, by listing those desired on the instructional schedule, the instructor can more adequately plan ahead and have appropriate ones developed in time, or obtain commercially prepared materials to meet the immediate needs.

Texts and References

Some courses or training programs are planned in such detail that each task listed will have a specific reference(s) listing. If this is true a column is provided so that the specific page listing may be entered opposite the appropriate task. This has advantages for both students and instructors in that both know exactly what content is to be learned.

In practice, however, this practice often becomes too time consuming for any one instructor to accomplish. The usual approach used is either to list text and reference readings for a cluster of tasks, or to list text and reference that apply to the total content included in the division or duty block of content.

Evaluation Devices

The listing of evaluation devices (tests, performances, exams, etc.) in a separate column usually occurs only when a great number are used throughout the particular offering. When this is done it is listed opposite the last tasks that will be included in the test, exam, etc. If evaluations are used rather infrequently, they are often listed as one of the last entries in the instructional schedule or below the instructional schedule format.

A number of advantages exist for listing the evaluation devices in the instructional schedule. First, this procedure provides the instructor with an indication as to when they will be used. Second, it provides the students with information as to exactly what will be included in the evaluation session and about when it will occur.

INSTRUCTIONAL SCHEDULE FORMATS

It will be found that there is no one correct type or kind of instructional schedule that will meet all of the demands of all course or training program offerings. Each instructor must design and develop a format that will meet the needs for the particular situation. Even though there are certain types of basic information that need to be included, the formats will still vary from instructor to instructor, from subject area to subject area, and from one teaching situation to another.

Figures 7-1 through 7-8 are example formats of instructional schedules. Each has the first four basic components (course title, division/duty, task, and time designation) included. Each, however, differs somewhat regarding the placement of the basic as well as the optional components. The first two formats, Figures 7-1 and 7-2, are partially completed.

The responsibility of the instructor is to select or design a suitable instructional schedule format to fit the specific offering. Of major concern is that the schedule fits the particular situation and includes the necessary information to help assure more effective instruction.

INSTRUCTIONAL SCHEDULE

INSTRUCTOR John Harris COURSE TITLE Drafting 1
TOTAL TIME 3 weeks DIVISION/DUTY Introduction

PROBLEMS	NO.	TASK DECRIPTION	CLASS M	CLASS I	CLASS A	INSTRUCTIONAL AIDS
	1.	Importance of drafting			x	Text, Chapt. 1
	2.	Identify and explain use of drafting tools		x		Text, Chapt. 2
	3.	Identify kinds of leads		x		Sample leads
	4.	Draw horizontal lines	x			Handout #1.1, 1.2
	5.	Draw vertical lines	x			
	6.	Measure with scale	x			
	7.	Layout borders	x			
Lettering plate	8.	Draw vertical letters	x			Lettering chart
	9.	Value quality of letters			x	
	10.					
	11.					
	12.					

FIGURE 7-1

INSTRUCTIONAL SCHEDULE

COURSE TITLE ___ Work Simplification ___

DIVISIONS/UNIT NO. ___ TITLE ___ Evaluating the Results ___ NUMBER SESSIONS ___ 2

NO.	TASK DESCRIPTION	TEXTS/REF.	AIDS	ASSIGNMENT	EVALUATION
1.	Describe cost analysis techniques	Engr. Handbook Chapt. 3	Transp. #4.1 Example #4.1 Handout #4.1		10 point quiz
2.	List and explain 5 step approach to a preferred method.				
3.	Identify and explain profit advantages from work simplification program.			Prepare cost savings report	
4.					
5.					

FIGURE 7-2

INSTRUCTIONAL SCHEDULE

COURSE TITLE _____ INSTRUCTOR _____
DIVISION/DUTY _____ LAB TIME _____ SHOP TIME _____

NO.	TASK DESCRIPTIONS	JOBS	AIDS	INSTRUCTION SHEET

ASSIGNMENTS

EVALUATION DEVICES

FIGURE 7-3

INSTRUCTIONAL SCHEDULE

COURSE TITLE _____ HOURS _____
DIVISION/DUTY _____ HOURS _____
INSTRUCTOR _____ LOCATION _____ DATES _____

NO.	TOPICS (TASKS) DESCRIPTION	AIDS-MATERIALS	ACTIVITIES-PRESENTERS

FIGURE 7-4

INSTRUCTIONAL SCHEDULE

COURSE TITLE ——————— TITLE ——————— TOTAL TIME ———————
DIVISION/DUTY NO. ———————

TIME	NO.	TASK DESCRIPTION	M	I	A	LAB EXPERIMENTS	AIDS	READINGS

FIGURE 7-5

INSTRUCTIONAL SCHEDULE

COURSE TITLE ——————— INSTRUCTOR ———————
DIVISION/DUTY ——————— TIME ———————

SESSION DATE	NO.	TASK DESCRIPTION	AIDS	HANDOUTS	READINGS	ACTIVITIES

EVALUATION PROCEDURE ———————

FIGURE 7-6

INSTRUCTIONAL SCHEDULE

COURSE TITLE _____ DIVISION/DUTY _____
TOTAL COURSE TIME _____ DIVISION/DUTY TIME _____

NO.	TASK DESCRIPTION	ASSIGNMENTS	PROJECTS-LABS	MATERIALS-AIDS

FIGURE 7-7

INSTRUCTIONAL SCHEDULE

COURSE TITLE ———————— TITLE ———— INSTRUCTOR ————————
DIVISION/DUTY NO. ————

NO.	TASK DESCRIPTION	TIME	CLASSIFICATION		
			MANIPULATIVE	INFORMATIONAL	ADDITUDINAL

ASSIGNMENTS ———————————————— EVALUATION ————————
REFERENCES ————

FIGURE 7-8

SUMMARY

The use of the instructional schedule provides the instructor with a means to organize materials for a selected offering into a very usable and concise outline. This schedule, in its comprehensive form, includes the listing of all the content and support activities and materials used by the instructor and for which the students are held responsible.

The instructional schedule provides a format for the sequential listing of learning tasks, shows a visual relationship of content and all support materials, provides an overview of the total course or training program, serves as an indicator for materials development, and provides a basis for long range planning, including the revision of the course or training program.

Four basic components must be part of every instructional schedule. These are, (1) course title, (2) division/duty designation, (3) a task listing, and (4) a time indication. An additional six components are necessary and recommended to form a comprehensive instructional schedule. These include: (1) list of methods to be used; (2) list of audio and visual aids; (3) activities such as projects, experiments, assignments, etc.; (4) written instruction sheet titles; (5) texts and references; and (6) a listing of evaluation devices.

The inclusion of the components in an instructional schedule, when properly entered, show a horizontal relationship which indicates those activities or learning content that are used together to further learning.

Many different formats have been used in the development of instructional schedules. There is no one correct format since it must be developed to fit particular needs, content, and situations. The major criterion is whether it will aid the instructor in conducting a more effective learning situation for the students.

SUGGESTED QUESTIONS AND ACTIVITIES

1. Explain why a listing of learning tasks in a sequential instructional order only is not as effective as a comprehensive course or training instructional schedule.

2. Compare a comprehensive instructional schedule with a course of study as to uses, advantages, and disadvantages.

3. List four reasons for developing and using instructional schedules. Justify each of these reasons.

4. Describe the difference between a lesson plan and the instructional schedule as used in a formal instructional setting.

5. Select a minimum of three components beyond those indicated as required for an instructional schedule. For each of these explain why it is important to include them in the schedule format.

6. In what ways will the instructional schedule format differ between a vocational and a general education oriented course offering.

7. For your instructional schedule, will you list specific tasks or list topic statements that include a number of closely related tasks? Why?

8. Why is it so important to include the time element in an instructional schedule? Is it more important for a beginning instructor?

9. Is it essential to have the auditory/visual aids and written instruction sheets developed before including them in the instructional schedule? Explain your answer.

10. Plan and develop two instructional schedule formats, one for an informationally oriented offering, and one for a manipulative oriented offering. Prepare a justification/explanation for the make-up of each.

11. For one division/duty of your course or training program, completely fill in an appropriate instructional schedule with all of the required entries under the components headings.

chapter 8

Lesson and Session Plans

The selection, sequencing, and detailing of tasks and the identification and development of instructional support materials need to be further organized beyond that of mere inclusion in an instructional schedule for effective instruction to result. The development of comprehensive lesson or session plans helps to bring all of these materials into focus and directed toward the accomplishment of selected learning tasks within a specified time frame.

Every instructor, no matter how competent and experienced, needs to plan the activities of each class session and to reduce this plan into writing. The lesson plan is the appropriate vehicle to be used in organizing the class session. It is the blueprint which assures that the instructor is prepared to teach; that everything to be taught is set down in the proper order; that the utilization of learning aids and devices, and references, has been provided for; and that little is left to change. The quality of preplanning determines the quality of the results.

Effective lessons do not just happen. They result from a great amount of effort and time by the instructor who desires to provide an appropriate learning environment for the dissemination of skills and knowledges. Regardless of how long an individual has been in the instructing profession, one should never attempt to make a presentation without a well planned and written lesson or session plan designed for a specific situation. Planning provides for the organization necessary for an effective presentation.

This chapter on lesson and session planning provides infor-

153

mation relative to the development of effective lesson and session plans. The major topics included are: (1) Importance and Use, (2) Lesson and Session Plan Criteria, (3) Lesson and Session Plan Formats, and (4) Writing the Lesson and Session Plan.

CHAPTER OBJECTIVES

Through the study of this chapter and the completion of the suggested questions and activities, you will have accomplished the following objectives. You will be able to:

1. List and explain the importance of lesson and session planning and their advantages, disadvantages, and uses.
2. List and describe the components of a comprehensive lesson or session plan, and the criteria used for lesson and session plan development.
3. List the nine steps in writing a lesson or session plan and state the purpose and procedure followed for each.
4. Write a comprehensive lesson plan for use in a particular course or training program.

IMPORTANCE AND USE

The organization of specific content to be offered during a particular time frame is one of the major problems facing all instructors and especially beginning instructors. A well thought out and developed plan will help to solve this particular problem. The lesson or session plan is actually a plan of procedure developed by the instructor to be used as a guide in presenting content and one that provides a learning environment for students. It may be referred to as a detailed part or section of a blueprint of the total instructional package.

The well developed lesson or session plan is of value not only to the instructor but also to the student, the supervisor, and the administrator. The value goes beyond that of merely knowing which steps come next in a particular presentation. It has value in that it provides a link for all the content included in a course. It is a means for instructional evaluation for coordinating content with other courses, and for making certain that adequate opportunities are provided students with the most effective means of learning the content.

Very carefully prepared lesson plans tend to structure a class to a great extent and even too rigidly at times. However, the lack of lesson planning would be more detrimental. An effective instructor will prepare the materials and the presentation outline to the degree of specificity to meet the particular needs at any given time.

Lesson or session plans are designed and developed so that the instruction will be maximally effective from the viewpoint of the instructor and have greater meaning for the students. The development of lesson or session plans is important for many reasons. Some of these include the following:

1. Provides a degree of standardization of instruction.
2. Presents a logical sequential listing of content.
3. Prevents over as well as under emphasis of selected content.
4. Provides a time schedule which serves as a guideline.
5. Causes instruction to follow accepted practices.
6. Causes instructors to analyze content prior to the presentation.
7. Provides a ready basis for revision.
8. Provides a record of content presented.
9. Coordinates component parts of the lesson.
10. Identifies specific content to be evaluated.
11. Provides for the listing of appropriate student activities that are directly related to the content presented.
12. Provides a list of aids, equipment, and references to be used.
13. Provides continuity between the lessons presented within a specific course.

For an instructor to merely have a list of information, skills, and facts concerning certain content is not enough. This information must be well organized and placed in a usable lesson plan format.

The nature of a specific lesson or session plan and its use is wholly dependent upon the needs, interests, and abilities of the students. The student rather than the time factor or class period should dictate the content included and length of the presentation. Also, the instructor must be aware that interest is essential and that the motivation factor must be considered.

LESSON AND SESSION PLAN CRITERIA

The lesson or session content and its resulting plan or format is selected, based upon certain criteria that should be considered in its development. Some of these criteria include the following:

1. Fits the particular content of the course.
2. Provides for adequate feedback.
3. Meets the needs of the student.
4. Meets the needs of the instructor.
5. Provides for student involvement at appropriate stages during the course of the lesson.
6. Focuses on a major point or concept to be learned of such a length that is comprehendible by the student, and preferably at one setting.
7. Contains something new and challenging to the student and which leads students to advanced learning.
8. Content is appropriate for the student and based on past experience.
9. Provision for proceeding from the known to the unknown.
10. Provides for accountability of student learning of the content.
11. Provides space for and shows relationship of all supporting instructional materials with tasks involved (i.e., aids, instruction sheets, etc.).
12. Is based on a "five step" presentation approach of instruction: (1) Introduction, (2) Presentation, (3) Application, (4) Summary and (5) Evaluation. (Each of these five steps is explained in detail in the section on Writing the Lesson and Session Plan.)

LESSON AND SESSION PLAN FORMATS

There is no one acceptable format that will fit all levels, content areas, student needs, or instructors' desires. Formats vary greatly due to a host of reasons. The major concern is that the particular format used fits the situation in question, it meets the needs of the student, the instructor, and the administrator. Each format should include components so that the plan will meet the lesson and session plan criteria presented in the previous section.

A lesson is not a time period but rather a body of cohesive content (learning tasks) to be presented as a unit so that greater learning occurs and the application will be more effective. Lesson planning, to be effective, includes and/or refers to all the information, data, activities, procedures, etc., that will be presented, discussed, and used during the period of time for which the lesson or session plan was developed.

Lesson and session plan formats are of two general types, comprehensive and abbreviated. The choice or selection of one or the other of these depends upon a number of factors; such as time available to conduct the lesson or session, the experience of the instructor, the nature of the content, the amount of standardization desired, and the requirements of the agency or institution.

Abbreviated lesson and session plans are often no more than content outlines listing some of the major steps, elements, or points included in each of the learning tasks that are to be presented. In many cases such components as aids, devices, and references are omitted. Abbreviated plans serve as interim documents to meet needs as they arise where time has been insufficient for more adequate planning. Figures 8-1 and 8-2 are two examples of abbreviated lesson and session plan formats.

Comprehensive lesson and session plans are developed by the instructor who will make the presentation. These plans are developed from learning task listings, course outlines or instructional schedules, where each of the learning tasks has been detailed to provide a carefully developed step-by-step procedure for presentation purposes. The comprehensive plan includes the listing or description of the exact subject content that the instructor will actually cover, as well as the listing of aids, materials, and other components and support materials

LESSON PLAN

COURSE _____ DIVISION _____
LESSON TITLE _____ NO. _____
OBJECTIVES:

    1.

    2.   (Objectives to be stated in performance form indicating
             expected behavior, condition, and performance level.)

    3.

PRESENTATION:

    (A listing of the major topics or procedures and sub-points
    that are to be covered in the presentation.)

REFERENCES:
    (References used for this lesson)

ASSIGNMENTS:
    (Specific assignments relating to this lesson)

FIGURE 8-1

SESSION PLAN

SESSION TITLE _____ DATE _____

INSTRUCTOR _____ DEPARTMENT _____

SESSION OBJECTIVES:

    1.

    2.   (Objectives to be stated in performance form indicating
             expected behavior, conditions, and performance level.)

    3.

SUPPORTING AIDS:

    1.

    2.   (List of all aids and devices to be used during the
             presentation.)

    3.

    4.

INTRODUCTION:

    (Refer to Step 3 in "Steps in Lesson and Session Plan
    Development")

PRESENTATION:

    (Refer to Step 4 in "Steps in Lesson and Session Plan
    Development")

APPLICATION:

    (Refer to Step 5 in "Steps in Lesson and Session Plan
    Development")

EVALUATION:

    (Refer to Step 7 in "Steps in Lesson and Session Plan
    Development")

FIGURE 8-2

to be used and considered in the specific lesson or session presentation. Comprehensive plans are hand tailored to fit specific situations. To develop them the instructor must carefully think through the total instructional sequence of the course, the relation to the students, the nature of the content, the facilities available, and the instructor's own capabilities. Figure 8-3 is an example of a comprehensive lesson format.

The specific components and format of a lesson or session plan may vary somewhat from one instructor and content area to another, but basically each plan format should include a number of components. Those plans containing all the components listed below in detail are considered to be comprehensive in nature, while those that contain only a portion of the listed components are to be considered to be abbreviated forms.

Each lesson or session plan should contain the following:

1. Course and division/duty identification
2. Lesson or session title
3. Lesson/session performance objectives
4. Presentation procedure
   a. Introduction to the lesson/session
   b. Presentation of content (the learning tasks)
   c. Application of content learned
   d. Summary of the presentation
   e. Evaluation of learning
5. Supporting learning aids, devices, equipment, materials, etc.
6. Assignments and readings for the present and the following lessons or sessions.

An instructor may find that the particular lesson or session plan may not be as effective as anticipated when it was originally prepared. If this is true, it should be revised immediately or as the instruction is presented. The format must be designed to fit the content, the student's needs, and the instructor's desires. The content and proposed procedures are not to be changed just to fit a particular lesson or session plan format.

Lesson and session plans serve as guides and assurances that relevant content is being considered and a logical and psychological approach is used. It is not something that is "set" for all time. As teaching situations change, so does the lesson plan; as the students change, so must the planning, and as the content changes so must the sequence of the sessions change.

WRITING THE LESSON AND SESSION PLAN

The writing of lesson and session plans should be done only after a great amount of preliminary work has been accomplished. These plans are based on the appropriate selection, sequencing, and detailing of learning tasks, accurately stated performance objectives, and the selection or development of supporting instructional materials. The plans should be developed only after a workable instructional schedule has been prepared.

Like any phase of educational or training program development, lesson or session planning involves a set of "trade-offs" or compromises. These might be in the form of time allowable for instruction, relationship between student abilities and the content, the ability of the instructor, and the philosophy of the institution in relationship to the particular course and lesson or session. The demands of the institution has a direct effect on the use of lesson and session plans as well as their make-up or format.

Some Considerations

Each lesson presented by an instructor usually contains from one to four learning tasks which have been identified through an instructional analysis of the subject or course. The number of learning tasks to include depends upon such factors as time available, complexity of the tasks, and the background of the students. The relationship between the lesson being prepared with those lessons presented earlier and those to come later must also be taken into consideration.

The relationship of a lesson or session plan to the total course must also be considered during its development. A single lesson must be considered as only one step in the total

LESSON/SESSION PLAN

Course No. ————————————
Division/Unit ————————————
Lesson/Session No. ——— Dates ———
Instructor ————————————

Lesson/Session Title ————————————————————————

Lesson/Session Objectives

Following the successful completion of this lesson/session, students will be able to:

1.
2.
3.
4.

(Objectives to be stated in performance form indicating expected behavior, conditions, and performance level.)

References Used:

1.
2.
3.

(References used for the preparation of this lesson/session plan, and those suggested for further study.)

Assignment for This Lesson:

1.
2.

(Specific assignments to be completed by the students.)

Aids/Devices Used.

1.   3.
2.   4.

(List of all aids and devices to be used during the presentation.)

1. Introduction Preparing the Student)

Sequenced Steps/Outline	Aids/Materials/Activities
(Refer to Step 3 in "Steps in Lesson and Session Plan Development")	(Suggested relevant aids, materials, and activities.)

FIGURE 8-3

2. & 3. Presentation & Application (Content presentation & Feedback)

Sequenced Steps/Outline	Aids/Materials/Activities
(Refer to Step 4 and 5 in "Steps in Lesson and Session Plan Development")	(Aids, materials, and activities to use and follow in the presentation and application step.)

4. Summary (Highlights of the lesson/session)

Sequenced Steps/Outline	Aids/Materials/Activities
(Refer to Step 6 in "Steps in Lesson and Session Plan Development")	(Additional aids, materials, and activities for summary highlights.)

5. Evaluation (Meet objective statements)

	Aids/Materials/Activities
(Refer to Step 7 in "Steps in Lesson and Session Plan Development")	(Evaluation aids, materials, and activities to use and follow.)

Next Lesson/Session Title:
Next Assignment:
   (Specific assignment for next lesson/session)

FIGURE 8-3 (Continued)

process of presenting the entire course. An effective lesson is developed out of a previous lesson and moves the student smoothly into the new lesson. Therefore, a single lesson usually has little value when considered only by itself; it must be combined with others.

In many courses, manipulative tasks and informational tasks along with attitudinal tasks are included. The three tasks, manipulative, informational and attitudinal, if very closely related, can and often should be presented during the same lesson or session period. However, each should be presented using the appropriate method or technique, showing students how these tasks are integrated so that they can grasp the meaning and have an understanding of the total concept(s) as stated by the lesson or session objectives.

The learning tasks identified to be included in a selected lesson or session are obtained from the sequential listing of the tasks in the instructional schedule. The determination as to whether the informational content in a specific lesson is to be presented before the manipulative content depends upon the background of the student, the preference of the instructor based upon experience, and the physical facilities available. The most important consideration is that a detailed listing of tasks and their respective elements or steps be made and their relationship shown and taught the student.

Steps in Lesson and Session Plan Development

Before actual lesson planning takes place, an assumption is made that the total course has been outlined, appropriate manipulative, informational, and attitudinal learning tasks have been identified (inventory of tasks) and sequenced for effective learning, and related learning tasks have been grouped, indicating those to be included in the same lesson or session. The steps presented below, with listed purposes and procedures, are generally followed in the order shown. However, depending upon the particular situation, the nature of content, the students and the instructor, the listed step sequence in planning may be changed. As these steps are studied, refer to Figure 8-3, the comprehensive lesson plan format.

Step 1. Identify and detail the learning tasks to be included.

Purposes and Procedures:
  a. Select appropriate learning tasks (manipulative, informational and/or attitudinal) from the instructional schedule.
  b. Select specific learning tasks which are closely related to be included in the same lesson.
  c. Determine time availability for the lesson, avoiding too long or too short sessions; usually include one to four learning tasks.
  d. Consider student background in selecting the number and kinds of learning tasks to be included.
  e. Tasks should be completely detailed, listing specific steps for each and supporting points of information.

Step 2. Write performance objectives

Purposes and Procedures:
  a. Review learning tasks to be included which form the basis for writing the performance objectives.
  b. Write objectives in performance form to include expected learner behavior at the end of the lesson, the condition under which the student will perform, and the level or standard of performance expected.
  c. Objectives are to relate specifically to the lesson being presented.
  d. May include a major objective with several supporting or enabling objectives, also written in performance form.
  e. Write all objectives in student terms; what they are expected to accomplish.

Step 3. Plan and write the "Introduction to the Lesson"

Purposes and Procedures:
  a. Considering students and content, plan how lesson will be introduced to be most effectual.

b. If it is the first lesson in the course, provide for introducing self and class members; develop rapport.

c. Develop student interest, curiosity, and provide for motivation.

d. Delineate the scope of the lesson and what is expected of the student.

e. Show students the value and importance of the content to be covered; stimulate desire to learn.

f. Explain the methods and techniques that will be used.

g. Ask questions, give examples, present related experiences.

h. Summarize previous lesson and give preview of upcoming lesson.

Step 4.* Plan and write the "Presentation of Content"

Purposes and Procedures:

a. Designed to provide specific instruction, the presentation of new ideas and skills.

b. List detailed steps included in each task to be covered, in logical and psychological learning order.

c. List aids, devices, and other supporting materials opposite each step (or task) where and when it will be used.

d. Include examples, illustrations, etc., to help clarify.

e. Place emphasis on key points and relate to applications.

f. Summarize each new concept/task presented before going on to the next one.

g. Identify and indicate specific methods or techniques to be used in presenting each task and task step.

---

*Most instructors combine steps 4 and 5 when developing their lesson plans because of their interrelatedness.

Step 5.* Plan and write the "Application of Content"

Purposes and Procedures:
  a. Provide for ways in getting students involved in the learning process.
  b. List questions to be used to obtain feedback to help evaluate effectiveness of lesson presentation and student comprehension.
  c. Provide opportunity for students to demonstrate manipulative skills presented, and verbal or written feedback following informational presentations.
  d. Plan for and list special activities, practice work, drills, etc., to be performed by students at appropriate times during the lesson presentation.
  e. Supervise work, check responses, correct errors.

Step 6. Plan and write the "Summary of Presentation:

Purposes and Procedures:
  a. List most important points (highlights) of the lesson presented as summary statements to be emphasized.
  b. Provide for clarity of total lesson and emphasize relationships of materials presented.
  c. Be specific and brief, and allow for and request questions from students.
  d. Relate content presented to stated lesson objectives.
  e. List assignments required and major points to be covered in the next lesson.

---

*Most instructors combine steps 4 and 5 when developing their lesson plans because of their interrelatedness.

Step 7. Plan and write the "Evaluation of Learning"

Purposes and Procedures:
   a. Determination of the extent of student learning is the major goal.
   b. Review stated lesson objectives which form basis of the evaluation.
   c. Determine type and kind of evaluation devices and procedures to be used.
   d. List specific items on which students will be evaluated.
   e. Provide for adequate evaluation sampling of content covered.
   f. List or include the evaluation instrument that will be used.
   g. May develop an evaluation procedure and instrument that will include several lessons.
   h. Determine efficiency of instruction and learning.

Step 8. Identify and list supporting materials (aids, devices, references, equipment, supplies, etc.)

Purposes and Procedures:
   a. Review detailed listing of steps for each task to be presented.
   b. Identify and list all supporting materials in appropriate places—opposite tasks and task steps (films, tapes, slides, transparencies, handouts, models, etc.).
   c. Identify texts and references related to the lesson content, including manual, etc.
   d. List all items of equipment, supplies, materials, aids, etc., to be used in appropriate sections of the format.
   e. Plan, develop and list assignment to be used.

Step 9. Complete lesson/session format

Purposes and Procedures:
   a. Enter information identifying the course, division/duty, lesson, dates, and instructor.

b. List lesson title, which should be brief but descriptive.
c. Review total lesson plan for completeness and continuity.
d. Plan the next lesson and list assignments.

Figure 8-4 summarizes the relationship between the specific procedural steps in developing the lesson or session plan and its place in the total instructional process.

THE LESSON/SESSION PLAN

	Planning Steps				
	1	2	3,4,5,6,7	8,9	
Instructional Schedule	Identify and detail tasks	Write objectives	Introduction Presentation Application Summary Evaluation	Select Supporting Materials Complete Form	Conduct lesson

FIGURE 8-4

SUMMARY

All instructors have an obligation to plan and organize each lesson or session in such a manner as to insure effective learning by their students. Effective lessons and sessions do not just happen. They are a result of careful planning by the instructor responsible for the specific presentation.

The planning and development of lesson and session plans is of importance to students, instructors, and administrators. Some reasons why these plans should be developed include: they increase standardization, present logical sequence, identify emphasis, provide a time table, promote use of an analysis, provide a record accomplishment, are a basis for evaluation, and provide continuity and relationships.

Certain criteria should be considered when developing lesson or session plans. Some of these are: they meet the needs of students and instructors, fit specific content and course requirements, focus on major concepts, contain something new, and are based upon the "five-step" presentation approach.

No one lesson or session format will fit all situations. Plans must be designed and developed to fit particular situations which vary with the type of content, of background of the students, and the orientation of the instructor and institution. Plans are of two general types, comprehensive and abbreviated. The comprehensive form is the most acceptable as it contains all the information needed for an effective presentation. However, it is the most difficult to prepare. Each comprehensive lesson or session plan contains the following six components:

1. Course and division/duty identification
2. Lesson or session title
3. Lesson/session performance objectives
4. Presentation procedure
   a. Introduction to the lesson/session
   b. Presentation of content (the learning tasks)
   c. Application of content learned
   d. Summary of the presentation
   e. Evaluation of learning
5. Supporting learning aids, devices, equipment, materials, etc.
6. Assignments and readings for the present and the following lessons or sessions.

The development or writing of lesson or session plans involves nine steps which should be followed for the plan to be effective. These steps are·

1. Identify and detail the learning tasks to be included.
2. Write performance objectives.
3. Plan and write the "Introduction to the Lesson"
4. Plan and write the "Presentation of Content"
5. Plan and write the "Application of Content"
6. Plan and write the "Summary of Presentation"
7. Plan and write the "Evaluation of Learning"

8. Identify and list supporting materials (aids, devices, references, equipment, supplies, etc.)
9. Complete lesson/session format

SUGGESTED QUESTIONS AND ACTIVITIES

1. From your observation, describe some of the results that occur when an instructor has not adequately planned a particular lesson or session.

2. Review the reasons given for the development of lesson or session plans. Rank the six most important ones and justify your decision. List any additional reasons that should have been included.

3. Develop a check list form containing the criteria of effective lesson/session plans that can be used in evaluating or in developing lesson and session plans.

4. Select a lesson plan which you or someone else has prepared. Apply the criteria presented in determining the suitability of the selected plan.

5. Compare the comprehensive and abbreviated lesson or session plan format on the points of (1) development, (2) advantages, and (3) use by beginning instructors.

6. Prepare an abbreviated form of a lesson or session plan which you plan to use for the course of study or training plan you are developing.

7. Prepare a comprehensive format of a lesson or session plan which you plan to use for the course of study or training plan you are developing.

8. What are some of the factors to consider when determining the number and kinds of tasks to include in one lesson or session?

9. Describe the relationship between the inventory of tasks, the instructional schedule, and the comprehensive lesson or session plan.

10. List the nine steps in developing the lesson or session plan. Explain how you plan to accomplish each step in your particular situation.

11. Write an abbreviated lesson plan to be used in your course or training program.

12. Write a comprehensive lesson plan to be used in your course or training program.

chapter 9

Written Instruction Sheets

W ritten instructional materials come in a variety of forms and serve a number of different purposes in the overall instructional program. Written instructional materials include all those materials in printed form, whether commercially or instructor prepared, such as texts, manuals, handouts, and instructor written instruction sheets.

The written instruction sheet, which is sometimes mistakenly referred to as a *handout*, is one form of written instructional material. It is different from many of the others because it is planned, developed, and used by the instructor to meet a specific situation and for specific students. To be effective, written instruction sheets are tailor-made to meet a need in courses or training programs when other commercially prepared materials are not available or applicable.

An instructor should consider the writing of instruction sheets only when other appropriately prepared materials are not available. The writing of instruction sheets consumes a great amount of time, something that most instructors have very little to spare.

This chapter deals only with instructor prepared written instruction sheets which are designed to assist in the more effective presentation of identified content in specific courses and training programs. The following major topics are treated: (1) Importance of Instruction Sheets, (2) Instruction Sheet Criteria, (3) Kinds and Uses of Instruction Sheets and (4) Writing Instruction Sheets.

CHAPTER OBJECTIVES

Through the study of this chapter and the completion of the suggested questions and activities, you will have accomplished the following objectives. You will be able to:

1. List and explain the major advantages and disadvantages in the development and use of instructor prepared written instruction sheets.
2. Identify, explain, and apply instruction sheet criteria, including required components, to writing instruction sheets and to evaluating possible effectiveness.
3. Describe the three kinds of instructor prepared written instruction sheets and explain the major functions that each is designed to serve.
4. Following the listed criteria and consideration for writing instruction sheets, plan and write comprehensive and brief instruction sheets that represent each of the three kinds of written instruction sheets.

IMPORTANCE OF INSTRUCTION SHEETS

For many years the unavailability of suitable up-to-date commercially prepared instructional materials forced instructors to prepare great numbers of instructional sheets to assist them in presenting technical information and skills. Today there is an abundance of texts, references, written materials, etc., that have been commercially prepared and designed for course and training program use. Many of these are excellent and, if used appropriately, further learning considerably. However, on the other side of the coin, many have been developed for sale and have questionable value, especially as related to specific local courses and training programs. It is for this latter reason that instructors must develop some of their own instruction sheets to meet their student's needs. This is especially true in instructional areas where the content changes quite rapidly. Also, instructor prepared instruction sheets are most essential when the student make-up in the course is heterogeneous or is unusual in some way, requiring the instructor to use a variety of approaches for content presentation.

A well prepared written instruction sheet is essential if it helps to clarify a concept, present a new idea, or reinforces what has already been presented. It does not take the place of the instructor, but rather supports the content being considered in a particular course or training program.

A well written instruction sheet, and one that is up-to-date, can often be used in later courses and training programs where like content is being offered. Instruction sheets are especially helpful for students who desire or need to progress at a rate different from the rest of the students. The instruction sheet combines information and directions which, when followed, provide students the opportunity to more effectively learn the concepts, facts, and/or satisfactorily complete manipulative skills.

Written instruction sheets are considered an important support segment to the instructor of any class whether primarily occupational or academic in nature. These sheets have a number of advantages as well as disadvantages as viewed by both the instructor and the students.

Advantages of Instruction Sheets

Some of the advantages of instructor prepared written instruction sheets include:

1. They are support materials for the instructor and aid in clarifying concepts and procedures presented by the instructor.
2. Provide for individualization, permitting students to progress at their own rate of speed in learning.
3. Assist in the conduct of large classes that include students of varying abilities.
4. Provide a means for recall of information and manipulative skill procedures which have been presented through other means.
5. A source of up-to-date content when other appropriate sources are not available.
6. Permit more of instructor's time to be spent working with individual students and small groups.

7. Place the major responsibility for learning on the student.
8. Help to develop a feeling of responsibility and self reliance in the students.
9. Are in permanent form so they can be revised and used for later offerings.
10. The use of written instruction sheets helps to establish a habit in students to seek out other information and procedures that are provided through printed and written form, such as manuals and technical references.
11. They supplement verbal instruction and are especially valuable where instructions are specific and lengthy.
12. Valuable to both slow and advanced students where used on an individualized basis.
13. Reduce excessive oral instruction covering content which is more effectively presented through written materials.
14. Cause instructors to more adequately organize their courses and training programs.
15. When written in appropriate language, they aid in avoiding misunderstanding which often occurs through verbal presentations and directions.
16. Are more closely related to what the student will face after leaving school, especially in their selected occupations.

Disadvantages of Instruction Sheets

Some of the disadvantages of instructor prepared written instruction sheets include the following:

1. They are quite difficult to prepare.
2. School duplicated materials are often not as appealing to students as commercially prepared materials.
3. Instructors tend to depend too heavily on the instruction sheets to do the teaching and forget to provide adequate personal instruction.
4. Learning of the content depends largely on the reading ability of the students.

5. Tend to structure the course or training program, thus prohibiting individual planning and creativeness.
6. Tend to reduce the opportunity for group activity, since most sheets are written for use by individual students.
7. Are too often written in such a way that it is difficult for students to understand them.
8. Many individuals have difficulty in interpreting printed instruction into application.
9. Students have a tendency to try all avenues available before they will read provided instruction sheets.
10. If students know they will receive written instructional materials covering certain content, they tend not to pay attention to instructor presentation.

Even though the above listed disadvantages to the use of written instruction sheets do exist, they may easily be overcome if the instructor is aware of them. The key to the effectiveness of instruction sheets and their use is student involvement, instructor awareness, and content that is up-to-date.

INSTRUCTION SHEET CRITERIA

Each kind of written instruction sheet might be considered individually for the identification of relevant criteria. However, there is so much similarity regarding the criteria that a basic set can be identified and used with some modification with any kind of written instruction sheet developed.

The criteria statements below should be considered as they might apply to any written instruction sheet being prepared by an instructor.

1. The language used should be appropriate and at the level of those who will use the instruction sheet. The language should be easily understood and, if possible, in conversational style.

2. Simplicity is the key word for the instruction sheet format. Complicated formats should be avoided in that they cause confusion and create a lack of clear understanding of the content. The instruction sheet should not be overcrowded.
3. Content should be presented to the point in a direct, straightforward manner, avoiding unnecessary information or statements not relevant to the specific content under consideration or the needs of the students.
4. Adequate and appropriate illustrations should be included that assist in communicating the concept, idea, or skill procedure. Illustrations save the use of many additional words.
5. Whether the instruction sheet is oriented toward providing information, describing a procedure, or presenting an assignment, it should make use of simple and short sentences which will encourage clarity and understanding.
6. Include all necessary explanations and directions for using the instruction sheet. This should include the purpose of the sheet and what is expected of the student in its use and completion.
7. The format used should be suited to the instructor's style and also be acceptable to the students. A minimum number of pages should be used since increased number of pages tend to cause decreased use by students.
8. Duplicated instruction sheets should be clear, legible, and attractive so as to not only present content effectively but also motivate students in their use.
9. All instruction sheets should be coded to assist in use and filing with other materials in a specific offering.
10. The organization of the sheet should include major sections with appropriate headings and sub-headings which help to present content in an orderly manner.
11. The thrust of the written instruction sheet should be designed to promote thinking and creativity on the part of the student.

12. The overall format and content of the written instruction sheet must be attractive, which will help to ensure its use.

Components of Instruction Sheets

It is difficult to list the components that all types of instruction sheets should contain to meet all of the specific needs in various instructional areas. However, there is a comprehensive set of components that should be considered for any instruction sheet regardless of its classification. The following are these components.

1. Written instruction sheet identification
   a. Type of sheet
   b. Course and division titles
   c. Class and instructor
   d. Coding designation
2. Title of content presented
3. General directions
4. Objectives—performance
5. References
6. Aids and supporting devices
7. Tools, equipment, materials, supplies, etc.
8. Procedural steps
9. Appropriate illustrations
10. Questions and evaluation procedures

The above listed criteria and essential instruction sheet components may also be used effectively in evaluating commercially prepared instruction sheets. A check list for developing and evaluating might be similar to the one shown in Figure 9-1 to be used with instructor prepared or with commercially prepared instruction sheets.

KINDS AND USES OF INSTRUCTION SHEETS

Over the years many different kinds of instruction sheets have been developed and used by instructors to supplement the available texts and references and their own presentations. The major concern of most instructors was to develop instruction sheets that would help them to be more effective so that greater learning would take place.

Written instruction sheets are grouped or classified in various ways based upon their primary use or purpose. Traditionally, these sheets were classified according to the type of content under consideration. Using this classification, instruction sheets have been grouped as follows: (1) Job Sheet, (2) Operation Sheet, (3) Assignment Sheet, and (4) Information Sheet.

EVALUATION OF WRITTEN INSTRUCTION SHEETS

Evaluator _____ Date _____

Kind of Sheet _____ Title _____

Prepared By _____ Prepared For _____

Circle the number to indicate your rating of the instruction sheet.

4 3 2 1 Language is appropriate to student's level.
4 3 2 1 Format is simple, complete, and easily understood.
4 3 2 1 Only relevant material is included.
4 3 2 1 Adequate and appropriate illustrations are included.
4 3 2 1 Adequate directions are provided.
4 3 2 1 Is clear, legible and attractive.
4 3 2 1 Is coded to course, unit, etc.
4 3 2 1 Contains appropriate heading and sub-heading.
4 3 2 1 Contains instruction sheet identification and title.
4 3 2 1 Includes a set of performance objectives.
4 3 2 1 Contains text and reference listing.
4 3 2 1 Lists aids and supporting devices.
4 3 2 1 Lists tools, equipment, materials, etc.
4 3 2 1 Includes procedural steps.
4 3 2 1 Provides for evaluation of student's progress.
4 3 2 1 Content contained is current.
4 3 2 1 Seems to have motivating qualities.
4 3 2 1 Content is valid.

Ratings

4 High   3 Above Average   2 Below Average   1 Missing

Draw a line through those items not applicable.

FIGURE 9-1

As additional technologies emerged and individuals representing other instructional areas became interested in developing and using written instructional sheets, additional names for special types of instruction sheets were introduced. Some of these include: (1) Project Sheet, (2) Procedure Sheet, (3) Activity Sheet, (4) Experiment Sheet, and (5) Problem Sheet. In many cases there were only slight differences between the more recent of these and earlier ones.

The major consideration for the development of these sheets is their use in supporting the instructor to provide the best learning opportunities possible. Although it is essential to identify the kind of instruction sheet to use in specific instances, of major importance is how they meet the purpose for which they were designed and developed, and how effective they are in the students' learning of content.

Kinds Of Instruction Sheets

It would seem that a more workable plan for classifying written instruction sheets would be one based on the *use* of the instruction sheet rather than on the nature of content or subject. This classification would be as follows: (1) Assignment Sheets, (2) Procedure Sheets, and (3) Information Sheets.

Assignment Sheet. The assignment sheet is designed and developed to assist a student in completing a particular assignment, which may be informational or manipulative content oriented or a combination of both. The essential characteristic of this type of sheet is that an assignment is made to the student for which the student is responsible for completing. This is one of the most valuable sheets since it does provide a maximum amount of student involvement and usually provides for flexibility so that changes can be made based upon student background, interest and ability.

The manipulative assignment sheet usually includes a listing of the tools, equipment, and materials required in the completion of the particular manipulative activity. In most instances it also includes drawings and illustrations along with specifications required for the completion of the assignment. The comprehensiveness and the amount of detail of the manipulative assignment sheet is usually reduced as the student becomes more advanced. Figure 9-2 is an example of a manipulative assignment sheet format.

The informational assignment sheet focuses on placing responsibility on the student to obtain the necessary informational content from suggested or provided resources. A major component of this particular sheet is a set of questions, of an application nature, so designed that students must study the suggested resources before being able to provide correct responses. Figure 9-3 is an example of an informational assignment sheet format.

Like the usage of all instruction sheets, the assignment sheet is used prior, during, and after instructor presentation. The instructor must explain the importance and use of the assignment sheet fully, and hold students accountable for their completion for the sheet to be effective.

Procedure Sheet. The procedure sheet is used when a specific and structured procedure is to be followed in completing a learning task or some routine procedure in class, laboratory, or shop activity. The instruction included in a procedure sheet must be very clear and easily understood by all students who are expected to follow it.

The procedure sheet may be thought of as a set of directions which is to be followed regardless of the student's ability, the kind of job, project, or experiment in which the procedure is included. Each task(s) identified through the analysis procedure and selected to be retained in a specific course or training program could be detailed and organized to fit into a procedure sheet format. In practice, however, this is not practical because of the time needed to detail each task and also because many procedures are already outlined in available texts, references and other resources.

No matter how carefully manipulative procedure sheets have been written, it is still necessary that the instructor demonstrates the particular procedure (task) to the students. Figure 9-4 is an example of a manipulative procedure sheet format which is based upon the detailing of selected learning tasks.

Procedure sheets may also be predominately informational in nature. These, like manipulative procedure sheets, must be explained fully by the instructor to the students even though the sheets present the procedure in great detail. As a student becomes more advanced, the procedure sheet may be less

MANIPULATIVE ASSIGNMENT SHEET

COURSE ————————— SHEET CODE —————————
DIVISION ———————— CLASS ———— DATE ————
INSTRUCTOR ———————— STUDENT ————————
TITLE ———(Specific title of sheet)———

DIRECTIONS

(The importance of and general directions for following, completing, and using the sheet.)

PERFORMANCE OBJECTIVES

(Specific objectives indicating expected student behavior, conditions, and performance level.)

REFERENCES/RESOURCES

(Suggested references and resources for additional study.)

TOOLS/EQUIPMENT   MATERIALS

(Tools and Equipment used in the assignment.)

(Materials used in the assignment.)

SPECIFICATIONS   PROCEDURAL STEPS

(Exact specifications to be met upon completion of the assignment)

(Specific list of steps to follow in completing the assignment, including appropriate and essential information. Steps often in form of task statements.)

ILLUSTRATIONS

(Appropriate illustration to clarify procedural steps.)

EVALUATION QUESTIONS/PROCEDURES

(A performance evaluation, model exhibit, etc., for student self use.)

FIGURE 9-2

INFORMATIONAL ASSIGNMENT SHEET

COURSE _____ SHEET CODE _____
DIVISION _____ CLASS _____ DATE _____
INSTRUCTOR _____ STUDENT _____
TITLE _____(Specific title of sheet)_____

DIRECTIONS

> (The importance of and general directions for following,
> completing, and using the sheet.)

PERFORMANCE OBJECTIVES

> (Specific objectives indicating expected student behavior,
> conditions, and performance level.)

ASSIGNMENT

> (Specific statement of assignment to followed in answering
> questions and/or completing the applications.)

REFERENCES/RESOURCES

> (References and resources to use in answering the questions
> and/or completing the applications.)

QUESTIONS/APPLICATIONS

> (Application type questions designed so that references and
> resources must be studied before answers or applications
> can be made.)

SELF EVALUATION

> (A suggested procedure and/or specific answers to questions
> and/or applications for self evaluation.)

FIGURE 9-3

MANIPULATIVE PROCEDURE SHEET

COURSE _____ SHEET CODE _____
DIVISION _____ CLASS _____ DATE _____
INSTRUCTOR _____ STUDENT _____
              TITLE _____(Specific title of sheet)_____

DIRECTIONS

(The importance of and general directions for following,
completing, and using the sheet.)

PERFORMANCE OBJECTIVES

(Specific objectives indicating expected student behavior,
conditions, and performance level.)

REFERENCES/RESOURCES

(References and resources from which procedure
was developed.)

TOOLS/EQUIPMENT   MATERIALS

(Tools and equipment used   (Materials to be used to
to complete procedure.)   complete procedure.)

PROCEDURAL STEPS   ILLUSTRATIONS

(Specific steps to follow   (Appropriate illustrations
in completing the pro-   to support and illustrate
cedure. Usually a pro-   the specific steps and
cedure in completing a   key points.)
specific manipulative
task along with key
points.)

EVALUATION

(Self administrative procedure to evaluate at various stages
in completing the procedure.)

FIGURE 9-4

comprehensive and detailed. Often the advanced student fills in or completes a procedure sheet developed in brief form which he then follows. Figure 9-5 is an example of an informational procedure sheet format.

Information Sheet. The major purpose of the information sheet is to present concepts and facts that help explain the why, when, and where about the content under consideration. It is prepared when such content is not available to the student or is not adequately presented through texts, references or other sources. The information sheet provides a source of information needed by the student that relates directly to the other activities required in the particular course or training program.

Information sheets differ from texts and references in that they contain only the essential content needed by the student in a specific course or training program in which the student is involved. This sheet is designed to supplement the content presented by the instructor, not replace it.

One of the major reasons for developing information sheets is that often the instructor is the only source for that particular information. The information sheet, therefore, helps to reinforce the content being presented by the instructor. It provides a record or resource that students can turn to for review and additional study.

Information sheets usually include one, two, or three informational tasks selected through the analysis procedure. The number of tasks included depends upon such factors as the complexity of each task and the background and competence of the student. The instructor must be careful, however, that not too much material is included in any one information sheet. As the length increases, the probability of the student reading it decreases. The content part of an information sheet should resemble that of a good technical article in a professional journal.

Figure 9-6 is an example of an information sheet format that is based upon the detailing of informational learning tasks.

Uses of Written Instruction Sheets

As stated earlier, written instruction sheets do not replace the instructor. Written instruction sheets are support

INFORMATIONAL PROCEDURE SHEET

COURSE _____ SHEET CODE _____
DIVISION _____ CLASS _____ DATE _____
INSTRUCTOR _____ STUDENT _____
                TITLE _____ (Specific title of sheet) _____

DIRECTIONS

> (The importance of and general directions for following,
> completing, and using the sheet.)

PERFORMANCE OBJECTIVES

> (Specific objectives indicating expected student behavior,
> conditions, and performance level.)

REFERENCES/RESOURCES

> (References and resources from which procedure
> was developed.)

INFORMATION POINTS   ILLUSTRATIONS

> (Specific points and sub-   (Appropriate illustrations
> points of informational   to clarify and support
> knowledge such as safety   information points and
> rules and procedures,   sub-points.)
> inspection points, test
> equipment usage, etc.)

EVALUATION

> (Self and instructor evaluation process to assure knowledge
> attainment.

FIGURE 9-5

INFORMATION SHEET

COURSE ——————————— SHEET CODE ——————
DIVISION ——————————— CLASS ————— DATE ————
INSTRUCTOR ——————————— STUDENT ——————————
TITLE ———— (Specific title of sheet) ————

DIRECTIONS

(The importance of and general directions for following,
completing, and using the sheet.)

PERFORMANCE OBJECTIVES

(Specific objectives indicating expected student behavior,
conditions, and performance level.)

REFERENCES/RESOURCES

(References and resources from which information was taken
and for further in-depth study.)

INFORMATIONAL CONTENT

(Informational content, not readily available to student from
other sources, developed and written by the instructor.)

ILLUSTRATIONS

(Appropriate illustrations
to clarify content.)

QUESTIONS

(Application type questions based on the informational content
presented.)

EVALUATION

(Procedure to follow in self evaluating answers to questions.)

FIGURE 9-6

materials and have their greatest value in providing another means for students to attain learning at their own rate of speed, an individualized approach. The instructor must be careful not to develop and use instruction sheets because it is thought to be the thing to do and everyone else is doing it. The use of an instruction sheet will be ineffective unless it communicates the content effectively, under consideration. In fact, teaching without instruction sheets is better than teaching with poor ones.

Since the value of a written instruction sheet depends upon whether it is read by the student, the sheet must be written with care, using the style and language which is both technically and student acceptable. Unfortunately, many students feel cheated if they do not receive some form of written materials covering the content discussed in their courses. However, the instructor must be careful not to merely hand out these sheets without following a well organized plan designed for their effective use. Experience has shown that too many instruction sheets are collected, filed and never used effectively by the students.

The instructor should carefully supervise the use of written instruction sheets during the student's first exposure to them. Like any other type of learning, first impressions are long lasting and tend to set the stage for their later use. Many students in the past have resented the requirement of their seeking knowledge and learning procedures from written materials, especially in laboratory and shop classes. This must be overcome for many reasons, one of which is that instructors do not have the time to provide personal and individual help for every student unless most of the routine and understandable information and procedures can be put in written form for those who can benefit from it.

The use of written instruction sheets should begin early during the first class sessions of every offering. When first used, each sheet must be explained in great detail. When procedure sheets are used, it is essential that the instructor follow the presented procedure step by step so students can see direct relationships and the value of the particular sheets being used. As the instructor does this several times, the use of the instruction sheet will become more acceptable to the students and will become a regular part of their educational process.

Written instruction sheets have limited value if students do not refer to them as problems or questions arise. The instructor should avoid answering questions directly and verbally if the problems have been treated adequately in the various instruction sheets. Students should be referred back to the appropriate written sheet whenever possible and practical.

A major factor to be considered in the effective use of instruction sheets is that of timing. It is important to determine when (during the session, day, etc.) the instruction sheet should be presented to the students, when it should be returned, etc. There is no one correct time for instruction sheet use. However, adequate time should be provided for full explanation by the instructor and time available for questions from the students. Each instruction sheet must be explained so that the student knows its purpose, what they are to do with it, and actions students are expected to take.

If possible, all of the information regarding how the sheet is to be used should be included in each written instruction sheet. Every written instruction sheet should have the characteristics of self-instruct materials. Following are some suggested procedures for using the three kinds of written instruction sheets.

Assignment Sheets. An acceptable procedure for using informational and manipulative assignment sheets might be the following:

1. Briefly introduce the content for which the assignment will be made.
2. Hand out the assignment sheet covering the content under consideration.
3. Explain the format and purpose of the assignment sheet, and the student's responsibilities regarding its use and completion.
4. Carefully explain each section of the sheet, providing time for student questions. Unless complete understanding is attained at this point, very little will be gained by its use.
5. If the assignment is primarily informational in nature (treating concepts, facts, problems, cases, etc.), and one which may take one or more class periods for completion, the instructor should:

      a. Make resources available or provide some direction to students where resources may be found.

      b. Require written responses, recording of data, or problem solutions.

      c. Use the assignment sheet and responses as a basis for discussion.

      d. Conduct an evaluation procedure (questions, tests, application, etc.).

6. If the assignment is primarily experimental or manipulative in nature (jobs, project, lab experiments, etc.) which do involve an extended period of time, the instructor should:

      a. Provide materials, tools, and other resources, have students provide them, or provide directions where they may be found.

      b. Indicate resources available, such as information and procedure sheets, texts, etc.

      c. Demonstrate manipulative skills when needed.

      d. Hold discussion periods (group or individual) regarding various facets of the assignment and the progress of jobs, projects or experiments.

      e. Use the assignment sheet as a record of progress.

      f. Use the assignment sheet along with the product produced, or experiment completed in the final evaluation.

Procedure Sheets. An acceptable approach for using a procedure sheet, one which is designed to provide steps in learning manipulative content or some classroom procedure to be followed, might be the following:

1. Briefly introduce the content or procedure to be considered.

2. Hand out the procedure sheet covering the particular manipulative content (task) or other procedure under consideration.

3. Explain the format and its purpose, and the student responsibility regarding its use and its completion.

4. If the procedure sheet presents a manipulative

task, the instructor should demonstrate it
following exactly the steps listed on the sheet.
5. If the procedure sheet presents some classroom or
   shop procedure that all students are to follow,
   explain each procedural step and reasons for their
   inclusion. Provide time for student study and
   follow with a question and answer period for
   purposes of emphasizing the importance of the
   procedure.
6. Require written responses to questions dealing
   with the procedure, the problems encountered,
   workmanship levels attained, etc., if appropriate.
7. Evaluate completed procedure using the procedure sheet as a basis along with tangible or
   intangible accomplishments.
8. Require students to retain sheets for future
   reference.

Information Sheets. An acceptable procedure for using an
information sheet which is designed to provide concepts, facts,
and ideas, might be the following:

1. Briefly introduce the content to be considered.
2. Hand out the information sheet covering this
   content, or a portion of it.
3. Explain the format and its purpose, and the
   student's responsibilities regarding its use (should
   require active student involvement).
4. Provide time for student reading, reacting,
   responding, etc. (during class or between classes).
5. Ask for written responses to questions and
   problems included on the sheet.
6. Use questions and problems as a basis of class or
   session discussion.
7. May follow up with some evaluation procedure.
8. Require students to retain sheets for future
   reference.

For the written instruction sheets to be used effectively
they must be pertinent to the specific content under
consideration. They must also become an integral part of each
session and not something added on and thus appearing to be

busy work for the students. Each written instruction sheet must have student involvment to be effective.

Instructors often explain that they will not use instruction sheets because students do not read them anyway. It is the responsibility of the instructor to not only develop well organized and attractive instruction sheets, but also to motivate students in their use. Most students will read well prepared and presented instructional materials. There is a relationship between the value and importance placed on written instructional materials by the instructor and the ultimate use of these materials by the students.

WRITING INSTRUCTION SHEETS

The writing of instruction sheets is one of the more difficult teaching tasks engaged in by the instructor. This is the reason for the recommendation that whenever possible the instructor select already prepared instructional support materials, prepared commercially or by other instructors, if they are directly applicable to the particular content being presented. However, from experience this does not occur too often. Because of this and also due to the unavailability of textbooks that adequately cover the content of an entire course or training program, it does become necessary to write selected instruction sheets to fill this void.

One of the greatest difficulties faced by the instructor charged with writing instruction sheets to meet particular content needs is that the instructor most frequently has not been trained nor has adequate experience in this type of writing. Instructors know what the content of each sheet should be but lack the ability to communicate effectively with their students through writing. Written instruction sheets must exhibit the best use of English grammar and sentence structure.

Some Consideration for Writing Instruction Sheets

The criteria presented in an earlier section should be considered when contemplating the writing of instruction sheets. Some additional helps are presented below:

1. The total sheet should be carefully planned before writing begins. This includes a complete outline or analysis of content to be included.
2. Statements to be included should be direct, brief and, when possible, in complete sentence form.
3. The use of the dictionary is important.
4. Content included must follow currently accepted practices.
5. It is recommended that a second method, approach, etc., should not be presented as this might be confusing, especially to the less knowledgeable students.
6. Be careful of copyright infringements.
7. Following the writing of an instruction sheet, request a knowledgeable person to read it and make constructive criticisms.
8. The number of pages for any one instruction sheet should be kept to a minimum. This depends upon the content as well as the type of students.

The writing of instruction sheets is most often done by the individual instructor who will be using them. However, in some cases a group effort in writing should be encouraged. This is especially true if a number of instructors are teaching the same courses or at least have competency in the same areas. It is also important that each is current in the technology, as well as having knowledge of the current literature and research in the field or area. However, the committee approach and instruction sheet writing can be deadly unless all individuals are dedicated and willing to spend considerable time and effort.

Effective instruction sheets are not only written but they are rewritten. Following the initial use of such a sheet, immediate revision should take place based upon student feedback, colleagues' suggestions, and the instructor's own reaction based on results attained.

Too often instructors do not develop and use their own sheets because of the time required in addition to their other teaching responsibilities. It should be remembered that the written instruction sheets, even though they are time consuming in preparation, are designed to provide more effective instruction rather than merely lighten the load of the instructor. Following the writing of the first instruction sheet, the next ones become easier and, in most cases, become more effective if based upon student feedback.

Steps in Writing Assignment Sheets

As indicated earlier, assignment sheets may be informational or manipulative oriented, or a combination of both. In most cases instructors develop these so that each sheet is either informational or manipulative. The basic steps for writing each are similar but do vary somewhat.

Information Assignment Sheet
1. Complete identification data such as course title, division title, code, etc.
2. State exact title of assignment sheet.
3. Write performance objectives to be attained through the completion of the sheet by the students.
4. List the resources to be used for completing the assignment.
5. Write general instructions or directions for completing the assignment and the accountability for it.
6. Develop and write out the exact assignment to be completed by the students including questions to answer and activities to complete.
7. Review sheet for clarity, relationships, organization and attractiveness.

Manipulative Assignment Sheet
1. Complete identification data such as course title, division title, code, etc.
2. State exact title of assignment sheet.
3. Write performance objectives to be attained through the completion of the sheet by the students.
4. Describe and explain the exact product, project, or experiment to be accomplished.
5. Write appropriate specifications, develop drawings and appropriate illustrations. (Students may

be required to develop their own specification and set of drawings.)

6. State approximate time required and costs involved. (Students may be required to calculate costs.)
7. List the tools, equipment, and materials needed to complete the assignment.
8. List the steps, in sequence, to be followed in completing the assignment. Add illustration, etc., where necessary (less comprehensive for advanced students).
9. List the tasks that will be learned in completing the assignment (optional).
10. Develop a set of questions designed to help evaluate performance at various stages and at the completion of the assignment.
11. Provide a list of references and other resources where additional information can be obtained.
12. Review sheet for clarity, relationships, organization, and attractiveness.

Steps in Writing Procedure Sheets

Procedure sheets, like assignment sheets, may be either information or manipulative oriented. In either case, the major purpose is to present a predetermined procedure to be followed by the student in the accomplishment of a task(s) or a routine. Tasks which have been detailed become the basis for the manipulative procedure sheets. The general steps in writing this type of instruction sheet are as follows:

1. Complete identification data such as course title, division title, code, etc.
2. State exact title of assignment sheet.
3. Write performance objectives to be attained through the completion of the sheet by the students.
4. List the tools, equipment and materials (where appropriate) needed to complete the procedure.
5. List the exact procedural steps to be followed

in completing the procedure. Add appropriate illustration where needed.
6. Develop a set of questions designed to help evaluate the completed procedure.
7. Include references used and those that may be referred to for further study.
8. Review the sheet for clarity, relationship, organization, and attractiveness.

Steps in Writing Information Sheets

Information sheets are designed to present information not readily available from other sources in a clear and straightforward manner. They are also written to help reinforce content which has already been presented verbally during the session. The general steps in writing this type of sheet are as follows:

1. Complete identification data such as course titles, division title, code, etc.
2. State exact title of information sheet.
3. Write performance objectives to be attained through the completion of the sheet by the students.
4. Develop a set of general directions to be followed in completing the information sheet and the accountability involved.
5. Write the content of information in a clear, understandable manner using appropriate headings and subheadings.
6. List the references and other sources used in developing the content.
7. Write application type questions to be answered.
8. Review sheet for clarity, relationship, organization, and attractiveness.

The comprehensiveness of each written instruction sheet depends upon the manner in which it will be used, the complexity of the content, the abilities of the students, and the instructor's intent. Often a portion of an instruction sheet is left blank for the student to complete. This is especially true for more advanced students. However, for beginning students, instruction sheets are generally very complete so that students become aware of what a good instruction sheet is and so that no important information or procedure is left to chance.

Duplication of Written Instruction Sheets

The instruction sheet may be very well written, following all the criteria listed for effective instruction sheets. However, if the duplication process used is not acceptable, much time and effort has been wasted. Each instructor must become aware of the duplication facilities available so that quality and quantity copies can be obtained at low cost and within a suitable time frame.

It is recommended that the least expensive and quickest duplication process be used for the sheets as they are first developed and used. Then, as they are revised, based upon feedback from colleagues and students and the changing technology, more permanent and more pleasing (which is usually more expensive) copies can be produced.

The ditto process is recommended for duplicating the first set of written instruction sheets. Following the revision, other acceptable processes include the mimeograph and offset. If very few copies are needed, the photocopy (Xerox) process is very acceptable.

The type of process used is dependent upon the institution's policies, financial resources, and available facilities. The instructor will need to operate within this framework.

SUMMARY

Instructor prepared instruction sheets are developed and used to meet specific course or training program requirements and students' needs that are not met by commercially prepared texts, references, and other written instructional materials. Instruction sheets do not replace but rather support the instructor in the presentation of concepts, facts, and manipulative skills.

There are a number of advantages to using instruction sheets. Some of these advantages include providing for individualization, clarifying concepts, aiding in the conduct of large classes, placing responsibility of learning on the students, supplementing instruction, assisting in organizing content, and helping to avoid misunderstandings. A number of disadvantages also exist. These include difficulty of writing, using sheets to avoid instructor preparation, a tendency to over-structure content and presentations, relying too heavily on student reading ability, and a tendency to inhibit individuality.

Well written instruction sheets meet certain identified criteria which include those of appropriate language, appropriate format and organization, adequate illustrations, specific directions for use, purpose and objective statements, and a direct relationship to the content being presented. Comprehensive instruction sheets contain the major components of instruction sheet identification; title of content presented; general directions; objectives; references; aids and supporting devices; tools, equipment, materials and supplies; procedural steps; appropriate illustrations; and questions and evaluation procedures.

All instructor prepared instruction sheets can be grouped into three classifications which are: (1) assignment sheet, (2) procedure sheet, and (3) information sheet.

The assignment sheet can be either informational or manipulative oriented, and is designed to assist students in completing particular assignments that provide for maximum student involvement. Procedure sheets, like assignment sheets, may include content that is either informational or manipulative. They are designed to present a specific structured procedure to be followed by students. The information sheet is designed to present concepts and facts that help to explain the why, when, or where about content under consideration.

The effectiveness of each kind of written instruction sheet is based upon how well the students understand its purpose and importance. Instructors must carefully explain each instruction sheet as it is introduced and emphasize the students' responsibility for its completion and the accountability involved.

Instruction sheets should be written only when other appropriate instructional materials are not available. Most effective written instruction sheets are ones prepared by the instructors who will be using them. Each of the three kinds of instruction sheets are written following a series of basic steps. The steps vary with the kind of instruction sheet being prepared.

SUGGESTED QUESTIONS AND ACTIVITIES

1. Do instructors write instruction sheets today for the same reasons that they wrote them 30 to 40 years ago? Explain.

2. Identify six advantages in using instructor prepared instruction sheets that you feel apply to your instructional situation. Explain why you selected these six.

3. Based on your readings and experience in using instructor and commercially prepared instruction sheets, prepare a criteria check sheet(s) to be used to evaluate (1) instructor prepared instruction sheets, and (2) commercially prepared instructional materials.

4. List and explain the major components of instructor prepared written instruction sheets. Compare this list and description with components included in instruction sheets used by you in the past.

5. For each of the three kinds of written instruction sheets presented in this chapter, complete the following: State (1) the major purposes, (2) levels where most effective, (3) type of content for which most applicable, and (4) major advantages and disadvantages of each.

6. Based upon your reading and experience, explain the relationship between the three kinds of written instruction sheets with the more traditional classification of instruction sheets.

7. Present reasons and justifications for initiating the use of written instruction sheets early in each course or training program offering. What difference does the kind of instruction sheet make regarding how soon it is introduced to the student.

8. Develop a step-by-step procedure for initiating and continuing use of each of the three kinds of instruction sheets for your particular course or training program. Explain the student accountability approach you will use.

9. List a set of considerations that should be reviewed beyond the criteria listed, when writing instruction sheets. Of these considerations, select the four you consider the most important.

10. Following the steps in writing instruction sheets, write one sheet each of the following for your course or training program: (1) informational assignment sheet, (2) manipulative assignment sheet, (3) manipulative procedure sheet, and (4) information sheet.

chapter **10**

Application and
Instructional Practices

The development of instructional materials, including the
course of study or training plan, has very little value
unless its components are organized in such a way as to form
a usable and coordinated instructional system designed to en-
hance and improve learning. The previous chapters have
provided guidelines and procedures to follow in the development of most of the components that make up a systematized
instructional program. An appropriate procedure in assembling these components is essential for the effective use of
these developed materials. A suitable check list should be
used when assembling prepared materials to help assure that
the course of study or training plan contains everything needed by the instructor and the student.

It is considered most important that the developer and, in
turn, the instructor be knowledgeable about the principles of
learning and teaching so that the most efficient methods may
be used for more effective instruction. The principles of
learning and teaching provide criteria and guidelines to be
followed in the application of materials developed for instructional purposes. Not only must the individual who is
responsible for instructional materials development and instruction be knowledgeable about learning and teaching
principles, but also the various techniques to be used in
presenting the various types and kinds of content.

With the diverse backgrounds held by students, it becomes
most essential that the instructional materials be developed in
such a way that instruction can be easily individualized. A
variety of approaches may be used for individualizing

instruction. These depend upon such factors as the nature of the content, age levels of students, competency levels of both students and instructors, available supplies and facilities, and the philosophy of the offering institution or agency.

A number of approaches for application of instructional materials and procedures regarding instructional practices are presented in this chapter. These should be viewed as suggestions and adapted to particular situations. The three topics presented in this chapter are: (1) Assembly of the Course of Study/Training Plan, (2) Learning and Teaching, and (3) Individualizing Content.

CHAPTER OBJECTIVES

Through the study of this chapter and the completion of the suggested questions and activities, you will have accomplished the following objectives. You will be able to:

1. Identify, describe and explain the purpose of each component and other items that form a comprehensive course of study or training plan.
2. Assemble a course of study or training plan for use in a specific instructional area and setting.
3. Explain the part that the instructor and the student must play to cause the learning and teaching environment to be effective.
4. List and explain the approaches and principles of learning and how these might be applied to the presentation of instructional content.
5. Identify and explain the nature of individualizing content and a number of selected approaches, their characteristics and present use.
6. Develop a self-instructional learning unit to include a selected number of tasks for a specific course or training program.

ASSEMBLY OF THE COURSE OF STUDY/TRAINING PLAN

The individual components of the instructional materials system are developed in such a way that the component content, and procedures used in its development, affect the other components, causing the course of study or training plan to be more or less effective. Following the development of the various components that go into making up a course of study or training plan, some organized plan must be initiated to assemble the materials so that they are usable and functional for a specific situation. As presented in Chapter 2, each course of study or training plan contains a minimum number of components. Along with these components, a number of other items are included to provide a cohesive and more usable course of study or training plan. Figure 10-1 presents a check list of items, including the components, to be considered and included in the final organization of the course of study or training plan.

A brief description of each of the check list items included in a course of study or training plan follows:

Title Page

This page contains a descriptive title of the course of study or training plan, one that is recognizable by those competent in that particular instructional area. The title page should, in most cases, include a designation of the institution or agency, department, date of preparation, and the name of the individual preparing the materials.

Table of Contents

The table of contents includes a listing of the major sections of the course of study or training plan. Page numbers should be provided so that the needed materials can be easily located. For ease of up-dating and providing for additions and deletions, each major section of the course of study or training plan may be given a letter or Roman numeral and all materials included in that section may be numbered consecutively. In this way, when a change is made, only that particular section's numbering system is affected.

Introduction

The introduction section describes for whom the course or training program is designed, the orientation or emphasis of

COURSE OF STUDY/TRAINING PLAN CHECK SHEET

_____ 1. Cover page

_____ 2. Table of contents

_____ 3. Introduction

   a. Course/program goals and purposes

   b. Nature and scope of the course/program

   c. Length and credit or units to be earned

   d. Grade level and type of students to be served

   e. Prerequisites and other entrance requirements

_____ 4. Division performance objectives

_____ 5. Instructional schedule

   a. Sequential and classified listing of tasks (manipulative, informational, attitudinal)

   b. Sequential listing of jobs, projects, problems, experiments and/or activities

   c. Sequential listing of support materials (texts and references, films, instruction sheets, evaluation devices, charts, etc.)

_____ 6. Prepared lesson or session plans

_____ 7. Prepared visual aids

_____ 8. Prepared instruction sheets

_____ 9. Prepared evaluation devices

_____ 10. List and sources of texts and references, films, charts, etc.

_____ 11. Prepared progress records and charts

_____ 12. Other support materials

FIGURE 10-1

the content, and the overall goals and purposes of the offering. The length of the course or program should be indicated and whether any credit or certificate might be awarded. This section also indicates the types of students for whom the content is designed, and the ability backgrounds and the prerequisites required of the students. This section defines the nature and scope of the total offering. It sets the stage for what is to follow. The philosophy and/or goals of the institution providing the offering may also be included in this section.

Division Performance Objectives

A set of performance objectives are prepared for each division of the course or program. These objectives which relate specifically to the particular division usually precede the instructional schedule for that division. The performance objectives must be clearly stated, student oriented, and attainable by the students.

Instructional Schedule

The instructional schedule, as described in Chapter 7, provides a very comprehensive outline of the course or program. Each new division begins on a separate page, which helps to facilitate up-dating of the course of study or training plan. The instructional schedule must contain the course and division title, the time needed to complete the division, a sequence of tasks (content), and a listing of support information and materials.

Prepared Lesson or Session Plans

The actual prepared lesson or session plans are usually placed just following the instructional schedule to which they apply. These may be brief or comprehensive, depending on the nature of the content, level and abilities of the students, and the competency of the instructor.

Prepared Visual Aids

Such aids as transparencies, drawings, pictures, etc., prepared to support specific content should, whenever possible, be placed within the course and following the instructional schedule to which they apply. Quite often various aids will be used that are too large, or for some other reasons will not be suitable for inclusion in the course of study or training plan. If this is the case, a special reference or notations should be indicated so that they will be available when needed during the instructional program.

Prepared Instruction Sheets

Whether commercial or instructor prepared, copies of appropriate instruction sheets are most often placed in the course of study or training plan following the instructional schedule to which they apply. It is also appropriate to include copies of actual handout sheets along with the more comprehensive written instruction sheets. The instruction sheets should be coded so that they may be easily filed or placed in the correct section and/or division.

Prepared Evaluation Devices

The various evaluation devices designed to evaluate student progress and instructor efficiency are also included in the course of study or training plan within the appropriate division. The criterion evaluation procedure approach is usually used. Copies of appropriate evaluation devices and procedures, developed and planned for evaluating manipulative, informational, and attitudinal content, are included.

List and Sources of Texts and References, Films, Charts, Etc.

The actual placement of the list that includes the above and their sources might be placed following the introduction section or following the instructional schedule section. This listing usually applies to all divisions and, therefore, is not repeated with each individual division. It is important that the source of the materials be included so that all data will be available for placing orders and for referral purposes.

Prepared Progress Records and Charts

For most instructional situations it is important that some means be developed for the recording and/or charting of student progress, whether this takes the form of grades, completions, competencies, etc. This is usually a more detailed and comprehensive format than the traditional grade book. The record or chart format may be quite similar to the analysis chart used in identifying content. The students' names are listed opposite jobs, projects, tasks, assignments, etc., that need to be completed and for which progress must be recorded.

Other Support Materials

For many courses and programs, support materials other than that already referred to are developed, prepared, obtained, etc., for use in the instructional setting. These materials are placed with other support materials to which they most nearly relate in meeting the student's and instructor's needs. Some of this type of support material and information might include classroom, shop, or laboratory layouts; listings of equipment, tools, and supplies; and personnel organizations.

For best results, the assembly of the course of study or training plan is organized in loose leaf form so that changes, additions, and deletions can be more readily made without disrupting the total package. Most instructors prefer to use 8½ x 11 sheets, punch holes, and assemble materials in a three-ring notebook. However, others prefer to divide their materials, somewhat according to the breakdown shown in Figures 10-2 and 10-3, and place in file folders for greater ease in filing and classroom or laboratory use.

It is best not to place prepared materials on paper or cards smaller than 8½ x 11 because of the need for all the space to include appropriate illustrations and other information; and

ASSEMBLY OF COURSE OF STUDY/TRAINING PLAN

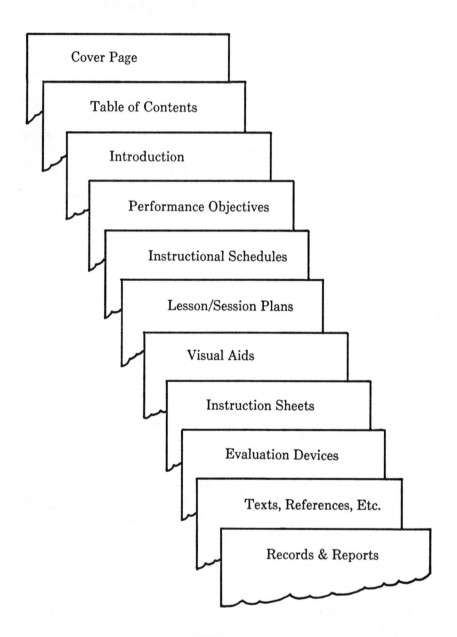

Cover Page

Table of Contents

Introduction

Performance Objectives

Instructional Schedules

Lesson/Session Plans

Visual Aids

Instruction Sheets

Evaluation Devices

Texts, References, Etc.

Records & Reports

FIGURE 10-2

ASSEMBLY OF COURSE OF STUDY/TRAINING PLAN

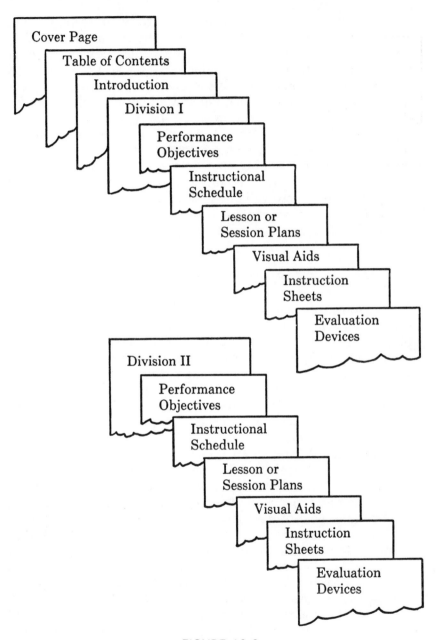

FIGURE 10-3

also to provide for making necessary changes as the materials are being used.

A very usable organized course of study or training plan would include items 1, 2, and 3 as shown in Figure 10-1, forming the first section of the course of study or training plan. This would be followed by separate sections for each division, which would include the division performance objectives, the instructional schedule, and all support materials for that division. The last section would be items 10, 11, and 12. Figure 10-3 illustrates this type of organization. Actually, there is no correct or incorrect manner in which to assemble a course of study or training plan. It must be assembled in such a way that it is flexible, readily up-dated, and can be easily used by the instructor. Figures 10-2 and 10-3 provide illustrations of two approaches that might be used in assembling the instructional materials developed.

LEARNING AND TEACHING

Principles of learning and teaching should have been considered when developing the course of study or training plan, which is based upon a scientifically organized and conducted analysis. The developer must be knowledgeable about how effective learning takes place, the relevant principles of learning, and the learning process. An instructor must have a grasp of the basic learning principles so that an effective instructional program can be presented. Selection of appropriate learning experiences is important. Learners expect and should demand an educational or training experience that is obviously relevant to them as they see it. The relevancy refers not only to the specific content items but also to the manner and means in which the content is presented.

The major goal of instructors is to provide the student with the special competency, through appropriate and relevant learning experiences, to perform effectively upon completion of the selected offering. The instructor should be concerned that the learner is more knowledgeable and skilled after having experienced the particular course or training session. Also, the attitude that a student holds toward the subject and the required experiences goes a long way in determining the use of the subject matter by the student in the future.

Appropriate and relevant education is that which provides an opportunity for students to attain a predetermined goal through verbal or abstract performance, or through manipulative activity using real objects. A number of specific ingredients must be considered regarding the relevancy of learning experiences. These include the instructor, the student, and the learning process or principles.

The Instructor

The instructor is the vital link between the technological world of tomorrow and the student of today. The instructor must assume the large part of the responsibility for the learning that takes place in the particular course or training program. The instructor must have the knowledge, background and experience, and the ability to identify, select, organize, and manage the instructional sequence so that it is relevant and meets the expressed needs.

It is essential for the instructor to communicate effectively with the students and provide for their individual differences. The instructor must review teaching skills, ability to utilize appropriate aids and devices, and ability to effectively evaluate the process as well as the product.

The instructor who expects to conduct an instructional program that is relevant, effective, and stimulating must be aware of some of the traits and factors that have often made learning difficult for students. These include the following:

1. Inadequate preparatory training for the specific teaching responsibility, technical and/or professional.
2. Out of touch with the "real" activities in which graduates of the program are involved.
3. Inability to get along and communicate effectively with students.
4. A lack of true interest in the subject being taught.
5. Impatience with the progress made by students with various levels of abilities.
6. Lack of ability to identify and organize instructional materials in a sequential manner for effective learning.

7. Lack of enthusiasm for not only presenting subject matter but also verifying the effectiveness of teaching.
8. Inability to present instructional material effectively using appropriate instructional aids.
9. An egotistical approach, resulting in domination of class and time, and possible eventual student resentment.
10. Conveying of "pet" ideas and convictions, resulting in a lack of relevant content coverage.

The teaching, which is performed by instructors, is actually organizing and directing the learning process. Learning occurs only when there is a change of behavior, which is accomplished by students through their own activities and experiences. Effective teaching influences students, resulting in emphasis on desirable learning and a de-emphasis on undesirable learning. The instructor must have the background and ability to determine what is desirable to fit certain situations.

An instructor who selects course content, sequences it, and eventually assembles a comprehensive course of study or training plan must always be concerned as to how the content will be accepted and learned by students desiring to attain competency in a selected phase of the subject matter. A great deal is known about learning that instructors can use. However, unless an instructor is knowledgeable about and accepts what is known about learning, very little change will be noticed in actual practice.

Probably one of the most important considerations for instructors is that they practice what they do know about learning even though they do not have complete knowledge of the various learning theories. Our concern is to provide an effective learning climate for students based on their needs, backgrounds, interests, and achievement levels.

The Student

Students who enter courses and training sessions bring with them certain attitudes, aptitudes, and an assortment of personal attributes that may aid or hinder them in learning the identified content. The attitudes that a student holds are actually what he thinks about himself, his chosen course, his ultimate goal, his surroundings, and his instructor. The aptitudes a student has will effect his ability to acquire the new content. Finally, the personal attributes that a student brings along to the learning situation include such things as patience, honesty, loyalty, courtesy and initiative. To some degree all students possess a combination of the various attitudes, aptitudes and personal attributes. For effective and relevant instruction to take place, the instructor must be aware of these and take them into consideration as the materials are organized for instructional purposes.

Students display certain characteristics of which the instructor must be aware so that effective and relevant instruction can be provided. These characteristics are displayed at different times by the same individuals and will change and/or be evident at different times during the student's life, through the various levels of education. Some of the characteristics that must be considered include the following:

1. *Curiosity.* In most cases, students desire to know the *what, why,* and *how* of things. Appropriate and relevant content helps to satisfy the curiosity of these students and more nearly assures that learning will take place.
2. *Constructiveness.* Students have the desire to create, to produce, and to achieve. Effective learning in most fields requires that students be provided with an opportunity to design, to produce, to diagnose, to repair, to disassemble, and to assemble.
3. *Identify.* It is the desire of all students to be visible and be recognized in the eyes of others. The lack of recognition has a direct affect on learning. Not only should content be relevant, but the student must be made to feel as important as the subject matter being presented.
4. *Dominance.* Students in the main enjoy and thrive on the mastery of specific situations. This includes the mastery of the specific content which has been identified and presented in particular courses and training programs.

5. *Competition.* The desire to excel is a characteristic of students who enjoy being in a learning environment and this characteristic must be used to effect greater and more effective learning. Various devices and approaches should be used to increase interest and promote increased effort on the part of the student.

6. *Orderliness.* In most cases the more interested students are concerned about orderliness and neatness. Learning, therefore, will be more effective and lasting if the instructor has his materials organized in an acceptable instructional order.

Learning Principles and Considerations

Effective teaching is very important to learning. A knowledge of the principles of learning is most valuable to the instructor and their application both in the selection of content and its presentation. Therefore, it is essential that the instructor makes use of what is known about the theories and the principles of learning.

Learning of content that has been scientifically obtained causes the learner to be different from others. The major purpose of learning is to make each person different from others and different from what they were before this learning occurred. Most effective learning occurs when it is built on that which is already known. Therefore, not only the selection of content is important but also its sequencing.

The concern is that the student changes behavior in three areas: (1) manipulative skill development, (2) technical information content, and (3) attitude for success in the present and future world of work. To effect changes in these areas, the instructor must have some knowledge of the principles of learning so that the content, which has been chosen as being relevant, might be presented in such a way that the educational experiences will be most easily and effectively learned.

Some principles of learning that must be considered in course of study and training plan development, which is based on a scientifically conducted analysis, include the following:

1. One learns the correct procedure or performance by becoming directly involved in performing.

2. One learns, and behaviors change, by responding to new stimuli.
3. One learns new content by associating it with content which has been effectively learned at an earlier time.
4. One learns most readily when one is vitally interested in the content being presented and is motivated by its seeming importance at the time.
5. One learns best when the surrounding environment has been especially organized and planned for effective learning.
6. One learns best when the specific content to be learned is reasonable in length and within the scope of one's abilities.
7. One learns best when the interest is high and the need is evident.
8. One learns most effectively when the content being presented is relevant and leads toward meeting one's ultimate objective.
9. One learns best when total concepts are presented, rather than individual and unrelated parts.
10. One learns best when more than one of the senses are appealed to by appropriate, strong, and relevant stimuli.
11. One learns best when previous pertinent learning experiences have been successful and chances of present learning experiences appear to have success factors included.
12. One learns best when opportunity is presented for application of that which has been learned in situations that appear relevant and which leads to one's ultimate objective.
13. One's learning is most effective when an opportunity is provided for adequate and appropriate repetition.
14. One learns more efficiently and effectively if one is held accountable for the learning.
15. One learns easier and more effectively if one is ready for the learning experience.

Instruction presented, to be effective, must be given in reference to the senses through which students learn. They do not learn equally well through each of these senses. The instructor must utilize those senses or a combination of senses considered most important to the individual student with reference to the particular content in question.

The senses through which learning occurs and those which must be considered when a real attempt is made to have instruction relevant include those of: (1) sight, (2) hearing, (3) touch, (4) smell, (5) taste.

As is shown in Figure 10-4, new knowledge is made up of manipulative, informational and attitudinal tasks which, in turn, are learned through the application of stimuli to one or more of the senses. It has been found that the largest portion of what we learn is through the sense of sight and second in importance is the sense of hearing. However, this may vary depending upon the nature of the content, as well as the abilities and background of the individual student. It is the instructor's responsibility to find the most effective method for learning as it relates to the combination of senses for the presentation of new knowledge.

In the main, students need the guidance and direction of instructors. Instructors have a learning impact on students, especially regarding the amount, kind, and quality of the content, and instructors can spur the student's interest in further learning of the particular subject. In the end, however, the student is responsible for the learning. The instructor cannot force individuals to learn or to change their behavior in a certain way; it is the student who does that.

LEARNING AND SENSES

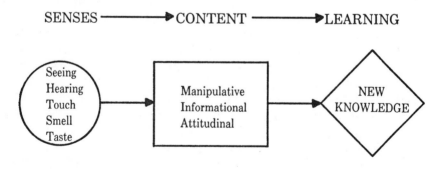

FIGURE 10-4

INDIVIDUALIZING CONTENT

When presenting instructional content, procedures should be developed and provisions made for individual differences in the classroom, the shop, and the laboratory. An obvious approach that might be used is to instruct only one student at a time, in some form of apprenticeship. This should provide the student with the most relevant type of instruction. However, this approach is not practical or economical. Therefore, other methods and approaches need to be developed and used so that greater individualization of content takes place.

The individualizing of instruction is not something new in education. Attempts have been made through the centuries by dedicated instructors to select and use methods and techniques designed to meet the specific needs of individual students. The fields of instruction which are of a practical nature lend themselves especially well to the individualized instructional approach.

Individualized instruction for its own sake has little merit, and only when it is initiated to help provide for the difference in individuals does it have value. This type of instruction may be especially necessary when individuals differ significantly in their cultural backgrounds, experiences, abilities, ages, and aptitudes. The instructor's ability, nature of facilities, levels of instruction, goals of students, and the specific type of educational program must be considered when planning for individualizing the instruction. Instruction which is individualized to make learning more relevant is a challenge to any instructor and especially one who not only manages a formal classroom but also conducts a shop or laboratory in a technological area that is changing from day to day.

Not only are individual differences considered when individualizing content, but also appropriate approaches and techniques used by instructors to meet the different needs and interests of students. Regardless of how expert an instructor may be in a technological field, failure will occur unless an understanding of the differences among students is known, and plans are made for class, shop, and laboratory instruction.

There are a number of approaches that an instructor may use in organizing, planning and managing instruction in the classroom shop or laboratory that will help in individualizing content. These approaches may vary from a detailed and comprehensive package of written and audio-visuals, to a more structured group approach with some attention given to individuals within the group. The following are a few of the more visible ways or procedures that may be used to more effectively individualize content.

1. Pairing of students
2. Films, slides, and tapes
3. Instruction sheets
4. Programmed books
5. Self-instructional learning units

Pairing of Students

The pairing of students is an approach used when some of the students, who have considerable competency in the content under consideration, are used to assist the instructor with those students who lack this competency. Care must be taken that the individuals get along with each other so effective communication has a chance of occurring.

The instructor must "check-out" the student who will be assisting to be sure that correct procedures will be followed and/or information presented. The problem of liability, responsibility, and authority should be considered and clarified so that an understanding exists.

One of the greatest advantages of this approach is that the students will tend to be more at ease during the learning session, thus providing for a greater amount of give and take, and questions and answers. This approach also gives the instructor more time to identify real problem areas. The instructor should be careful not to rely too heavily on this approach and expect the more competent students to do all of the instructing. It must be remembered that these students are only assisting in the total learning environment, and cannot and should not have the final authority regarding the learning process.

Films, Slides, and Tapes

The use of films, slides, and/or tapes have frequently been

thought of as a cure-all for presenting content on a group as well as use on an individual basis. These can be most effective if proper plans have been developed so that their use actually does aid in providing an individualizing approach.

The mere possession of relevant films, slides, and tapes does not assure that individualized instruction will take place. Special procedures must be planned for this to happen. The film, slide series, and/or tape must be of such length that interest can be maintained by the student. These usually include several selected and closely related tasks for each showing or use

For more effective use on an individualized basis, special handouts should be prepared that will cause the student to interact with the film, slide series, and/or tapes. This handout should contain pertinent questions to which students are to answer and statements that require student application of the content learned through the film, slides, and/or tapes.

The usual procedure is to have the student stop the presentation at predetermined places at which time responses, applications, etc., take place. If possible, suggested answers are provided the student after which the next concept, procedure, idea, etc., is presented. This continues until the presentation is completed. After completion, some form of evaluation usually takes place which, if possible, should be student administered.

Instruction Sheets

The use of instructor prepared written instruction sheets is one of the most effective and practical approaches for the instructor to use to provide for the individualization of content. Regardless of the type of instruction sheet (Assignment Sheet, Procedure Sheet, or Information Sheet), if properly developed will aid the student in gaining competency on a more individualized basis. Chapter 9 presents a detailed description of the kinds of instruction sheets, their uses, their characteristics, and their advantages and disadvantages. A review of Chapter 9 will provide a guide for use of the written instruction sheets to more effectively individualize the learning situation.

For written instruction sheets to be most effective in individualizing content, they must contain the components listed in Chapter 9. Each instruction sheet containing the appropriate components will provide the student with the directions necessary for completing the sheet, the resources needed for study or performance, and will demand the appropriate student involvement and evaluation.

Written instruction sheets are especially valuable for advanced tasks and topics. Since reading ability and comprehension are essential for effective student use of the instruction sheets, the reading level must be appropriate for the students. When properly prepared and administered, written instruction sheets can also be very effective as a remedial instructional tool.

Written instruction sheets are support materials primarily and, therefore, should be used to support the instructor's presentation rather than replace it.

Programmed Books

A large number of programmed books produced commercially are available in most of the technical and skilled areas for a nominal price. Care must be taken that the content has direct relationship to the course or training program (the identified and selected tasks). Too often programmed books are purchased without first checking the content, which may be too elementary, too advanced, or not relevant to the content under study.

The programmed books are either of the *linear approach,* where the student must progress from simple to complex, completing all of the content, or the *branching approach,* where the student may progress more rapidly by omitting content already known. Regardless of the approach, the student must be able to read with understanding and be knowledgeable of the terminology included.

The writing of programmed books by the instructor is both difficult and time consuming. However, it is time well spent for those content areas which are basic and will be used by a large number of students. It should be remembered that the program should not be too lengthy, which might cause a loss of the student's interest and motivation.

Involvement by the student is absolutely essential, which means that the student must respond to questions or make applications. Also, an immediate feedback must be provided in the form of answers to questions, quality measures, and/or appropriate evaluations by the instructor. As in the case with other individualizing approaches, information and content should be obtained from available commercial sources whenever possible to help reduce the time required by the instructor in developing the required materials.

Self Instructional Learning Units

The development of self-instructional learning units is another approach used by instructors to help individualize content. This approach includes all materials that are needed in one package or it might refer the student to selected resources to obtain the necessary information, directions, or applications. The student is totally responsible for the program, including (in most cases) the evaluation of his attained proficiency.

The components that make up a self-instructional learning unit vary somewhat based upon the nature of content, the philosophy of the instructor, and the abilities of the students. Basically, however, each self-instructional learning unit should contain the following components:

1. *Introduction and General Directions.* This component includes the general procedure to be followed in completing the learning unit. It may also indicate the prerequisite required, the place it occupies in the course, and other information relative to its identification.

2. *Performance Objectives.* The performance objectives statement indicates exactly what is expected of the student and the required performances. Each learning unit package usually contains several objectives which are written for the tasks (two to four closely related tasks) included. If the student already has the competency indicated in the statement, the procedure is to take the pre-test or move directly to the criterion post-test.

3. *Pre-Test.* Before the student is required to get involved in any of the resource materials, an opportunity is given the student for showing the competencies already possessed. The pre-test can be oral, written, performance, or a combination of

the three. Quite often the performance objectives are written and presented so that they serve a dual function, that of the objective statement and the pre-test. Regardless of the approach taken, the pre-test should be self-administering if at all possible and should take a minimum amount of time.

4. *Resources.* The resources component includes all of the material necessary to complete the learning unit, a part of the materials and additional references, and/or a referral to other sources from which knowledge and skill procedures can be obtained. For most instructors, the approach used is to refer students to other available resources and only develop their own as a last resort. This is because of the considerable amount of time required to develop appropriate resource materials. When possible, a student should be given the opportunity to select from several resources, the ones that best fit the situation.

5. *Criterion Post-Test.* Following the completion of the pre-test or the study of the resources, the student must complete the criterion post-test. This test is based on the stated performance objectives which cover the content to be learned by the student. The criterion post-test may be identical to the pre-test; however, in most cases it is more comprehensive and greater in depth. The criterion post-test is an indication to the instructor of the actual competency which the student has.

6. *Application.* The application component is concerned with how well the student can apply what has been learned to an actual situation. This component can be an extension of the criterion post-test in some situations. Its major purpose is to assure the student and the instructor that the content learned can be applied to an on-going project or assignment.

An example of a partially completed format, including the six components, is shown in Figure 10-5.

Some characteristics that should be considered when attempting to effectively individualize content in the classroom, laboratories and shops include the following:

1. Content must have been obtained through appropriate analysis procedures so that it is highly relevant.
2. The tasks must be detailed into steps and both the tasks and the steps sequenced to provide a logical and psychological approach to learning.

3.4 WRITING PERFORMANCE OBJECTIVES

MODULE LEARNING UNIT 3.4
(3 clock hours)

Introduction

This learning unit on Writing Performance Objectives is designed for all instructors regardless of the instructional area. First, read the objective statements listed below. If you feel that you are competent in these, then . . . .

Objectives

After successfully completing this unit, you should be able to:
1. Accurately differentiate between goals, performance objectives and tasks.
2. . . . .
3. . . . .

Pre-Test

1. Explain the major reasons for writing performance objectives.
2. . . . .
3. . . . .
4. . . . .

Resources

Read and study two of the following three resources:
1. Mimeograph handout
2. . . . .
3. . . . .

Post-Test

Following the completion of the resource material study, obtain the post-test, complete it, and check your answers . . . . . .

Application

1. Write performance objectives for a selected lesson you plan to present.
2. . . . .

FIGURE 10-5

3. Content must be available or presented in small units (tasks) so that evaluation can be effectively carried out and progress easily determined.
4. Student involvement must be provided and built into the presentation approach, whether designed for individual use or for group use.
5. Feedback must be built in so that it will function for the individual learner as well as for the instructor.
6. The developed materials to be used must be carefully prepared so that the procedures and content are communicated effectively to the students.
7. Specifically stated performance objectives must be prepared so that a course of action can be planned and the expected performance level achieved.
8. Progress by individual students must be identifiable at any time, based on the abilities and background of the student.
9. Evaluation procedures should be developed so that evaluation can be done on an individual basis, not dependent upon the total class.
10. Adequate assistance must be available to each student, when and where needed, so as not to hinder progress.

A simplified graphic illustration, including the basic components of an individualized approach, is shown in Figure 10-6.

INDIVIDUALIZED APPROACH

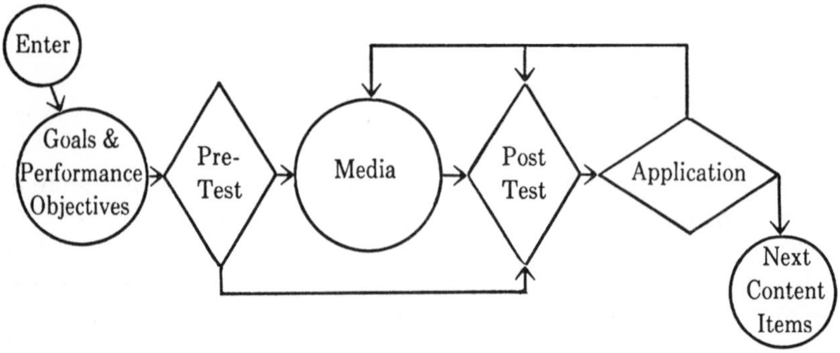

FIGURE 10-6

Many advantages occur to the student through the use of individualized approaches in the classroom, laboratories and shops. Some of these benefits include the following:

1. Students have an opportunity to learn new content based upon their readiness to learn.
2. Progress of each student is based on the student himself or herself rather than on the performance of the total group.
3. A greater amount of instructor time is available for work with individual students.
4. Any one student's progress will not hinder any other student's progress.
5. Progress becomes an individual matter.
6. Evaluation and feedback are integral parts, thus providing continual knowledge of student progress and a chance for revision to meet changing needs.
7. Individualized instruction provides for a guided learning system within the framework and controlled by the goals and objectives which are determined by the instructor and/or student.
8. Such instruction also provides a built-in flexibility which tends to be less detrimental to the student.
9. Permits more time for an instructor to become a diagnostician and resource person.
10. The student is given a chance for building self confidence regarding content without too much interference from other students.
11. The element of failures is reduced.

SUMMARY

The assembly of the course of study or training plan combines the instructional materials components. This should be done in such a way that the materials are usable and functional for a specific situation. A check sheet should be used to help assure that all necessary information is included. The prepared course of study or training plan should be so organized that changes can be made easily. Materials may be kept in a loose-leaf notebook format or kept in folders, with each division and its support materials in one folder.

The major goal of instructors is to provide the student with the required competency through appropriate and relevant learning experiences. For more effective learning to take place, the instructor should be knowledgeable about the principles of learning and the techniques of teaching. It is essential that the instructor communicates effectively with the students and provides for their individual differences. There are some traits of instructors which cause learning to be more difficult for the students. These must be taken into consideration when initiating the course of study or training plan. The background and experiences of students also need to be considered for most effective use of the course of study or training plan. These include such items as attitudes, aptitudes, goals, competencies, and interests.

Instruction is more effective if it is individualized to meet the needs of individual students. The individualization of content is not new; however, some of the techniques presently used are relatively new to many instructors. Some procedures and ways of individualizing that can be used effectively in the classroom, shop, and laboratory, include pairing of students; films, slides, and tapes; use of instruction sheets; programmed books; and self-instructional learning units.

The pairing of students consists of the more competent students serving in the role of an instructor assistant. Films, slides, and tapes assist in individualizing content especially when their use is planned so that forced student involvement occurs. Written instruction sheets are very effective for individualizing content when written by the instructor and prepared so student response and evaluation becomes an integral part. Programmed books use either the linear or branching approach. They are difficult to construct and, therefore, are more often purchased than instructor prepared. The use of self-instructional learning units is probably one of the most effective ways to individualize content. They are relatively easy to prepare by the instructor and, when containing the appropriate components, provide for total student involvement, including self-evaluation.

SUGGESTED QUESTIONS AND ACTIVITIES

1. Explain how the introduction section of the course of

study designed for general orientation would differ from one included in a training plan.

2. List the advantages and disadvantages of assembling a course of study or training plan in a notebook format; in file folder format.

3. Make a list and describe what might be included under the heading of "other support materials" listed on the check sheet.

4. Develop a plan you will use in assembling your instructional materials. Explain how you will use this approach in specific instructional areas.

5. Explain the meaning of "the instructor is the vital link between the technological world of tomorrow and the study of today."

6. Compare the listed instructor traits with those you have that might help cause lack of effective communications with students. Compare these traits with those of other known instructors.

7. React to the following statement: "The only evidence we have that learning has taken place is if there is a change in behavior by the students."

8. Explain why it is desirable to put current theories or principles of learning into practice through your course even though you may not fully understand the theories or principles.

9. Characteristics of students, to some extent, determine the organization and presentation of content. Explain why this is true. Provide some examples of this happening.

10. Select five specific learning principles which you support. Observe several instructors for the purpose of identifying if they put these principles into practice. Indicate how.

11. Explain what individualization of content means from the point of view of the instructor; the student.

12. Prepare a presentation involving a film or a slide/tape series. Develop necessary materials and a procedure that will effectively individualize content using the approach.

13. Obtain a programmed book for your technical area. Evaluate this book on the basis of relevancy, clearness of presentation, purpose, level, and students for whom it is designed.

14. Of the five approaches to individualizing content presented, which one or ones will be most effective for you? Support your answer.

15. Develop a detailed plan for using each kind of instruction sheet in your course that will help individualize the content and place the learning responsibility upon the student.

16. Explain what is meant by self-instructional learning units. List the advantages and disadvantages of using this approach for individualizing content.

17. Develop several self-instructional learning units for your content that include all of the components listed.

Index